THINKING
ABOUT THE
LONGSTANDING
PROBLEMS
OF
VIRTUE
AND
HAPPINESS

▼

Essays, a Play,
Two Poems and a Prayer

TONY KUSHNER

NICK HERN BOOKS

1995

The following essays were published previously in a slightly different format
(see essays for detailed publication information): "American Things" *Newsweek;*
"Fick oder Kaputt!" *Esquire;* "A Socialism of the Skin (Liberation, Honey!)" *Nation;*
"With a Little Help from My Friends" *New York Times;* "Some Questions About
Tolerance" *Monographs;* "Copious, Gigantic, and Sane" *Los Angeles Times.*

Because of space constraints on this page, bibliographic information for
quoted material within this book is detailed on page 227.

Printed in the United States of America

A CIP catalogue record for this book is available from the British Library

ISBN 1 85459 228 9

Cover: Komar & Melamid's "A Knock at the Door" reprinted courtesy of
Ronald Feldman Fine Arts, New York, Private Collection. Photo: D. James Dee.

Book and cover design by Lisa Govan

When beyond noise of logic I shall know
And in that knowledge swear my knowledge bound
In all things constant, never more to show
Its head in any transience it has found:
When pride of knowledge, frames of government,
The wrath of justice gagged and greed in power,
Sure good, and certain ill, and high minds bent
On destiny sink deathward as this hour:
When deep beyond surmise the driven shade
Of this our earth and mind my mind confirms,
Essence and fact of all things that are made,
Nature in love in death are shown the terms:
When, through this lens, I've seen all things in one,
Then, nor before, I truly have begun.

—JAMES AGEE
"Sonnets"

CONTENTS

PREFACE

I'm a playwright, not an essayist or a poet or a preacher.
But on various occasions, since *Angels in America*, I've
either been called on or been inspired to try forms other
than plays. Perhaps the works gathered here are simply
dramatic monologues masquerading as poems or essays;
perhaps they only work if you read them aloud, or better
yet, have them read aloud by talented actors. Perhaps the
whole collection is *really* a long, experimental play, with
Slavs! as a narrative interlude. Try declaiming the essays to
an audience; you will feel like you are being bar or bas
mitzvahed.

I notice that I catalogue a lot, I make lists of things,
mostly of bad things. In Sarah Schulman's beautiful new
novel, *Rat Bohemia*, a character says, "There is not enough
anger for everything that makes me angry." As Judaism
teaches, you have to be worried about everything evil, all
at once, all the time. That's what God expects of you.
Making lists is one way of doing that, of not excluding,
not forgetting.

I prefer to pontificate from behind my characters and
the fictions through which they romp and argue. But it's

probably a healthy thing, revealing the man behind the curtain. Behind that man, of course, there is another curtain, and another man behind *that*, and so on. I believe that the playwright should be a kind of public intellectual, even if only a crackpot public intellectual: someone who asks her or his thoughts to get up before crowds, on platforms, and entertain, challenge, instruct, annoy, provoke, appall. I'm amused and horrified when I realize that, on occasion, I'm being taken *seriously*. But of course being taken seriously is my ambition, semi-secretly-and-very-ambivalently held. I enjoy the tension between responsibility and frivolity; it's where my best work comes from.

As is the case with practically everything I write, I am indebted to Kimberly Flynn, in innumerable exchanges with whom my ideas and my styles and my sense of the world at large are largely shaped. I explain more about my intellectual relationship with Kimberly in the essay "With a Little Help from My Friends." More people have responded to this essay, which appeared in the *New York Times*, than any other I've written, suggesting, perhaps, that the issues it addresses—indebtedness and collaboration—are of general concern. Thanks to the people who have told Kimberly they liked my work, and her part in it. (Please, everyone, stop calling her a "muse.")

Thanks, also, to Joyce Ketay and Carl Mulert, my agents, to my sister Lesley, to my brother Eric, to my father, to my aunt Martha, to my whole supportive extended family and to a large number of friends; but in this book I'm especially grateful to Mark Bronnenberg, Kathy Chalfant, Oskar Eustis, Deborah Glazer, Brian Kulick, Craig Lucas, Jim

Magruder, Michael Mayer my girlfriend, Ellen McLaughlin my angel and fellow writer, Jim Nicola, Lisa Peterson, Michael Petshaft, Stephen Spinella, Tony Taccone, Tess Timoney, Rosemarie Tichler and George C. Wolfe.

Terry Nemeth and the folks at TCG have been generous, encouraging and indulgent to a fault, but no fault I'd ever care to name. I appreciate their work more than I can say.

SPECIFICALLY, I want to thank editors Will Blythe at *Esquire*, Allison Silver at the *Los Angeles Times* and Aric Press at *Newsweek*, all of whom were great to work with. Andrea Stevens at the *New York Times* has been a pleasure, a treasure, a wonderful editor, and supportive and encouraging throughout the past two years, and I'm very grateful. Katrina vanden Heuvel, the late and much-missed Andrew Kopkind and JoAnn Wypijewski at the *Nation* have been colleagues, comrades and collaborators—and I owe the title of the essay "A Socialism of the Skin (Liberation, Honey!)," as well as its final shape, to JoAnn.

Wendy Lesser's suggestions and reading of this manuscript, and her erudition, friendship and encouragement, have been tremendously important. Everyone should rush out and subscribe to the *Threepenny Review*, the country's best literary magazine.

ESSAYS

▼

AMERICAN THINGS

Summer is the season for celebrating freedom, summer is the time when we can almost believe it is possible to be free. American education conditions us for this expectation: School's out! The climate shift seductively whispers emancipation. Warmth opens up the body and envelops it. The body in summer is most easily at home in the world. This is true even when the summer is torrid. I have lived half my life in Louisiana and half in New York City. I know from torrid summers.

On my seventh birthday, midsummer 1963, my mother decorated my cake with sparklers she'd saved from the Fourth of July. This, I thought, was extraordinary, fantastic, sparklers spitting and smoking, dangerous and beautiful atop my birthday cake. In one indelible, ecstatic instant my mother completed a circuit of identification for me, melding two iconographies, of self and of liberty: of birthday cake, delicious confectionery emblem of maternal enthusiasm about my existence, which enthusiasm I shared; and of the nighttime fireworks of pyro-romantic Americana, fireworks-liberty-light which slashed across the evening sky, light which thrilled the heart, light which exclaimed loudly in the thick summer air, light which occasionally tore off fingers and burned houses, the fiery fierce explosive risky light of Independence, of Freedom.

Stonewall, the festival day of lesbian and gay liberation, is followed closely by the Fourth of July; they are exactly one summer week apart. The contiguity of these two festivals of freedom is important, at least to me. Each adds piquancy and meaning to the other. In the years following my seventh birthday I had lost some of my enthusiasm for my own existence, as most queer kids growing up in a hostile world will do. I'd certainly begun to realize how unenthusiastic others, even my parents, would be if they knew I was gay. Such joy in being alive as I can now lay claim to has been returned to me largely because of the successes of the political movement which began, more or less officially, twenty-five years ago on that June night in the Village. I've learned how absolutely essential to life freedom is.

Lesbian and gay freedom is the same freedom celebrated annually on the Fourth of July. Of this I have no doubt; my mother told me so, back in 1963, by putting sparklers on that cake. She couldn't have made her point more powerfully if she'd planted them on my head. Hers was a gesture we both understood, though at the time neither could have articulated it: "This fantastic fire is yours." Mothers and fathers should do that for their kids: give them fire, and link them proudly and durably to the world in which they live.

One of the paths down which my political instruction came was our family Seder. Passover, too, is a celebration of Freedom in sultry, intoxicating heat. (Passover actually comes in the spring, but in Louisiana the distinction between spring and summer was never clear.) Our family read from Haggadahs written by a New Deal Reform rabbinate which was unafraid to draw connections between Pharaonic and modern capitalist exploitations; between the exodus of Jews from Goshen and the journey towards civil rights for African-Americans; unafraid to make of the yearning which Jews have repeated for thousands of years a democratic dream of freedom for all peoples. It was impressed upon us, as we sang "America the Beautiful" at the Seder's conclusion, that the dream of millennia was due to find its ultimate realization not in Jerusalem but in this country.

The American political tradition to which my parents made me an heir is mostly an immigrant appropriation of certain features and promises of our Constitution, and of the idea of democracy and federalism. This appropriation marries freedom—up-for-grabs, morally and ideologically indeterminate freedom—to the more strenuous, grave and specific mandates of justice. It is the aggressive, unapologetic, progressive liberalism of the thirties and forties, a liberalism strongly spiced with socialism, trade unionism and the ethos of internationalism and solidarity.

This liberalism at its best held that citizenship was bestowable on everyone, and sooner or later it would be bestowed. Based first and foremost on reason, and then secondarily on protecting certain articles of faith such as the Bill of Rights, democratic process would eventually perform the action of shifting power from the mighty to the many, in whose hands, democratically and morally speaking, it belongs. Over the course of two hundred years, brave, visionary activists and ordinary, moral people had carved out a space, a large sheltering room from which many were now excluded, but which was clearly intended to be capable of multitudes. Within the space of American Freedom there was room for any possibility. American Freedom would become the birthplace of social and economic Justice.

Jews who came to America had gained entrance into this grand salon, as had other immigrant groups: Italians, Irish. Black people, Chicanos and Latinos, Asian-Americans would soon make their own ways, I was told, as would women, as would the working class and the poor—it could only be a matter of time and struggle.

People who desired sex with people of their own gender, transgender people, fags and dykes, drag kings and drag queens, queers, deviants from heterosexual normality were not discussed. There was identity, and then there was illness.

I am nearly thirty-eight, and anyone who's lived thirty-eight years should have made generational improvements on the politics of his or her parents. For any gay man or lesbian since Stonewall, the politics of homosexual enfranchisement is part of what is to be added to the fund of human experience and understanding, to the cosmologies, described and assumed, that we pass on to the next generation—upon which we hope improvements will be made.

The true motion of freedom is to expand outward. To say that lesbian and gay freedom is the same freedom celebrated annually on the Fourth of July is simply to say that queer and other American freedoms have changed historically, generally in a healthy direction (with allowances for some costly periods of faltering, including recently), and must continue to change if they are to remain meaningful. No freedom that fails to grow will last.

Lesbians and gay men of this generation have added homophobia to the consensus list of social evils: poverty, racism, sexism, exploitation, the ravaging of the environment, censorship, imperialism, war. To be a progressive person is to believe that there are ways to actively intervene against these evils. To be a progressive person is to resist Balkanization, tribalism, separatism, is to resist the temptation to bunker down; to be progressive is to seek out connection. I am homosexual, and this ought to make me consider how my experience of the world, as someone who is not always welcome, resembles that of others, however unlike me, who have had similar experiences. I demand to be accorded my rights by others; and so I must be prepared to accord to others their rights. The truest characteristic of freedom is generosity, the basic gesture of freedom is to include, not to exclude.

That there would be a reasonably successful movement for lesbian and gay civil rights was scarcely conceivable a generation ago. In spite of these gains, much of the social progress, which to my parents seemed a foregone conclusion, has not yet been made, and much ground has been lost. Will racism prove to be more intractable, finally, than homophobia? Will the hatred of women, gay and straight, continue to find new and more violent forms of expression, and will gay men and women of color remain doubly, or triply oppressed, while white gay men find greater measures of acceptance, simply because they are white men?

Along with the principle of freedom, much that is gory

and disgraceful is celebrated on the Fourth of July, much that is brutal and oppressive. American history is the source for some people of a belief in the inevitable triumph of justice; for others it is the source of a sense of absolute power and ownership which obviates the need to be concerned about justice; while for still others American history is a source of despair that anything like justice will ever come. The can-do liberalism of an earlier day may be faulted for having failed to consider the awesome weight of the crimes of the past, the propensity for tragedy in history, the river of spilled blood that precedes us into the future.

The tensions that have defined American history and American political consciousness have most often been those existing between the margin and the center, the many and the few, the individual and society, the dispossessed and the possessors. It is a peculiar feature of our political life that some of these tensions are frequently discussed and easily grasped, such as those existing between the states and the federal government, or between the rights of individuals and any claim society might make upon them; while other tensions, especially those which are occasioned by the claims of minorities, of marginalized peoples, are regarded with suspicion and fear. Listing the full catalogue of the complaints of the disenfranchised is sure to raise howls decrying "victimology" and "political correctness" from those who need desperately to believe that democracy is a simple thing.

Democracy isn't simple and it doesn't mean that majorities tyrannize minorities. We learned this a long time ago, from, among others, the demi-Moses of that Jewish-American Book of Exodus, Louis Dembitz Brandeis, or in more recent times from Thurgood Marshall. In these days of demographic shifts, when majorities are disappearing, this knowledge is particularly useful, and it needs to be expanded. There are in this country political traditions congenial to the idea that democracy is multicolor and multicultural and also multigendered, that democracy is about returning to individuals the fullest range of their freedoms, but also about the sharing of power, about the rediscovery of collective responsibility. There are in this country political traditions—from organized labor, from the civil rights and black power movements, from feminist and homosexual liberation movements, from movements for economic reform—which postulate democracy as an ongoing project, as a dynamic process. These traditions exist in opposition to those which make fixed fetishes of democracy and freedom, talismans for Reaction.

These traditions, which constitute the history of progressive and radical America, have been shunted to the side, covered over in an attempt at revisionism that began during the McCarthy era. Over the course of American history since the Second World War, the terms of the national debate have subtly, insidiously shifted. What used to be called liberal is now called radical; what used to be called radical is now called insane. What used to be called reactionary is now called moderate, and what used to be called insane is now called solid conservative thinking.

The recovery of antecedents is immensely important work. Historians are reconstructing the lost history of homosexual America, along with all the other lost histories. Freedom, I think, is finally being at home in the world, it is a returning—to an enlargement of the best particulars of the home you came from, or the arrival, after a lengthy and arduous journey, at the home you never had, which your dreams and desires have described for you.

I have a guilty confession to make. When I am depressed, when nerve or inspiration or energy flags, I put Dvořák's Ninth Symphony, *From the New World*, on the CD player; I get teary listening to the Largo. It's become classical Muzak, one of the all-time most shopworn musical cliches, which I think is regrettable. My father, who is a symphony conductor, told me that Dvořák wrote it in Spillville, Iowa. The National Conservatory of Music brought him to America to start a nationalist school of American composers. Dvořák contributed all the money from the *New World* Symphony's premiere to a school for former slaves. But then his daughter fell in love with a Native American from the Spillville reservation and Dvořák freaked and took the whole family back to Bohemia.

Like many Americans, I'm looking for home. Home is an absence, it is a loss that impels us. I want this home to be like the Largo from the *New World* Symphony. But life most frequently resembles something by Schoenberg, the last quartet, the one he wrote after his first heart attack and they had to stick a five-inch needle into his heart to revive him. Life these days is played out to the tune of that soundtrack. Or something atonal, anyway, something derivative of Schoenberg, some piece written by one of his less talented pupils, something else.

The only politics that can survive an encounter with this world, and still speak convincingly of freedom and justice and democracy, is a politics that can encompass both the harmonics and the dissonance. The frazzle, the rubbed raw, the unresolved, the fragile and the fiery and the dangerous: These are American things. This jangle is our movement forward, if we are to move forward; it is our survival, if we are to survive.

This essay was first published in the June 27, 1994 issue of Newsweek.

FICK ODER KAPUTT!

Fick oder kaputt.
(Fuck or die.)

—SHIRLEY STOLER'S SS OFFICER TO
GIANCARLO GIANNINI'S COCKROACH/
SURVIVOR IN LINA WERTMULLER'S MOSTLY AWFUL
(BUT NICELY FILMED) *SEVEN BEAUTIES*

In sex you swallow maybe a quart of someone else's spit. Sorry to be indelicate, but you do. It is the stream of want and need and hunger and fantasy and curiosity you plug into when you plug into a partner who knows what it is to kiss. Friction is dry and friction in sex can be very nice but sooner or later you want Flow, you want the juice in the berry; sex may begin arid, cool and delicately perfumed but will end up floating saltfunky in a tidal pool.

At any other time spit's nasty, but when you kiss it is . . . well, nectar, nepenthe, gone over from spit to nepenthe in a transubstantiation more divine than that accomplished in any Holy Mass. There is such a weary, wonderful feeling after a good fuck: La Tristesse, some sort of

13

fragile, metaphysical, post-coital bodily grief over the loss of self, the little death echoing the big one; or maybe that's too French. Maybe it's just the body's attentions momentarily diverted: the body preoccupied with all this Wondrous New Flora and Fauna you have introduced it to, a happy gardener weeding out the bad, letting the good take root. And sometimes from your lover you catch delicious little colds . . . in the bygone days of yore.

Yes, AIDS, of course. I am a homosexual, after all, and from now until the day they learn how to target gay baby fetuses and abort us all in utero (Kidding! But why do you think they're so hot to find the gay gene or gay interstitial hypothalamic brain cell or whatever if not to Out us and then Off us before we're whelped?), no gay man can ever again speak about sex without everyone's thoughts, including his own, performing contrapuntal meditations on morbidity and mortality. This is right and this is good but then again duty being duty is not release so it's sort of a drag, but then again life and the preservation of life is more important even than sex, isn't it? Isn't it?

Yes, *of course* it is. (And then on the other hand I feel duty-bound to report this: Several of us in a bar one night, we'd all been in psychoanalysis or at least psychotherapy and none of us was more than ordinarily crazy yet we agreed: We will learn to suck cock with a rubber if we have to and wash that vulcanized flattening chemical aftertaste out afterwards, and it *is* hard to wash away, isn't it, or is that just me; but if they decide that kissing isn't safe then fuck it, we'd all rather be dead. We were oral types, maybe that's the problem, and some of us showed it—fat. And here we were saying life was impossible without kissing, and I think that's true, don't you?)

(And some people don't even like to kiss, which I cannot comprehend. All sex is a pretext for a chance to kiss. And of course, to cum. And of course to work out and work through or perhaps merely to *practice* issues of submission and dominance, or whatever. It is impossible to talk or write about sex without revealing too much of yourself. Whereas conversely it is possible I think to *have* sex and reveal nothing of yourself whatsoever.)

Sex is like learning to eat like a grownup, to savor rather than enjoy, and you learn the *complicated* pleasures, pleasures that may challenge the palate and require reflection, contemplation, to recognize as delectables. I am revealing too much of myself. But I mean so what if Michel Foucault liked titclamps now and then, who doesn't (oops!); I mean, who except for a few tired straight-boy academics who should all go out and have themselves a forgodsake genuine limit experience before getting all *worked up* about it. Oh God I hope my *father* doesn't read this.

But *is* sex or life more important? Some people faced with the choice choose never to touch again, or become incapable of anything other than frottage and they frott and they frott until that becomes tired and they are *over* it, and it becomes tired quickly. And then I suppose they will either lapse from the arid back into the fluid, whence all life springs (and this is true even if the fluid is germy) (and all fluid is), or simply cease sexual activity altogether, and that is a choice too but not one I could ever make. Am I weak?

Sex has brought me joy. My people, my community defined by desire. The sweet Joy of Belonging. These are the honeyed leavings of my longings. Sex can be anaesthetic and awakening, abject and exalted, retaliatory and kind, dismal, angelic and pathetic, and all at the same time sometimes—sort of like the twenty hours of the *Ring Cycle* compressed into a few minutes thrashing on a bed. I think I ought to give sex up, I think I ought to invent an ascetic life and then live it because sex *distracts* and *torments* and in the nineties *frightens* me so; and I think probably letting go of the worst of sex is the key to aging well; and also I am overweight and so I'm not getting it as much as I used to, so to give it up would be . . . would be. . . . But I am damned, Sam Nunn, I am damned. (Sam Nunn. How did *he* get in here? Did he ask? Am I telling? And what is his problem anyway, who died and made *him* Jesse Helms? Jesse Helms didn't die, that's for sure; they promised us he would and then he didn't.)

I am assuming since you read *Esquire* you might be straight, but sit by me anyway; I'm not a bigot. I read *Esquire* when I was a boy—well, I didn't *read* it, I flipped to the back part and ripped out the underwear ads when the barber wasn't watching, slipped them into my pocket where they burned like petals of flame till I got them home and enflamed myself. Those *pouchy* men. What I did with those ads then is between me and God, and She isn't telling but it wasn't sex, for sex is not something you do alone.

When life no longer presents the occasion for sex it should present the near occasion; that is, we should talk about it endlessly and debate issues like monogamy/chastity/restraint versus fucking everything (consenting, adult) that moves, and the political and cultural valences of these choices; talk with open minds, realizing that talking about sex is dangerous because talking about sex makes us want to do it.

I for instance can be ever so butch or the distilled essence of swish as the mood moves me but *talk* about sex and the queen in me buds and flowers, and she spreads her muumuu across the worn aubergine velvet of her couch: her jeweled, tapered, *experienced* hands. . . . Come sit by her. In the air are the soft sibilants and susurrations, the whispered syllables and invitations, the words that wend serpentine towards perdition or redemption; and the liquid flow of breath; and everywhere suddenly there is a generosity and an opulence and a drama arisen out of nothing, and this, this my darling, is the magic of sex.

This essay was first published in the October 1993 issue of Esquire.

A SOCIALISM
OF THE SKIN
(LIBERATION, HONEY!)

Is there a relationship between homosexual liberation and socialism? That's an unfashionably utopian question, but I pose it because it's entirely conceivable that we will one day live miserably in a thoroughly ravaged world in which lesbians and gay men can marry and serve openly in the army and that's it. Capitalism, after all, can absorb a lot. Poverty, war, alienation, environmental destruction, colonialism, unequal development, boom/bust cycles, private property, individualism, commodity fetishism, the fetishization of the body, the fetishization of violence, guns, drugs, child abuse, underfunded and bad education (itself a form of child abuse)—these things are key to the successful functioning of the free market. Homophobia is not; the system could certainly accommodate demands for equal rights for homosexuals without danger to itself.

But are officially sanctioned homosexual marriages and identifiably homosexual soldiers the ultimate aims of homosexual liberation? Clearly not, if by homosexual liberation we mean the liberation of homosexuals who, like most everyone else, are and will continue to be oppressed by the depredations of capital until some better way of living together can be arrived at. Are homosexual marriages and soldiery the ultimate, which is to say the only achievable aims of the *gay rights movement*, a politics not of vision but of pragmatics?

Andrew Sullivan, in a provocative, carefully reasoned, moving, troubling article in the *New Republic* a year ago [May 10, 1993], arrived at that conclusion. I used to have a crush on Andrew, neo-con or neo-liberal (or whatever the hell they're called these days) though he be. I would never have married him, but he's cute! Then he called me a "West Village Neil Simon," *in print*, and I retired the crush. This by way of background for what follows, to prove that I am, despite my wounded affections, capable of the "restraint and reason" he calls for at the opening of his article, "The Politics of Homosexuality: A New Case for a New Beginning."

Andrew divides said politics into four, you should pardon the expression, camps—conservative, radical, moderate and liberal—each of which lacks a workable "solution to the problem of gay-straight relations." Conservatives (by which he means reactionaries, I think, but he is very polite) and radicals both profess different brands of an absolutist politics of "impossibilism," which alienates them from "the mainstream." Moderates (by which he means conservatives) practice an ostrich-politics of delicate denial, increasingly superseded by the growing visibility of gay men and lesbians. And liberals (moderates) err mainly in trying to legislate, through antidiscrimination bills, against reactive, private sector bigotry.

Andrew's prescription is that liberals, with whom he

presumably identifies most closely, go after "pro-active" governmental bans on homosexuals participating in the military and the institution of marriage. Period. "All *public* (as opposed to private) discrimination against homosexuals [should] be ended and . . . every right and responsibility heterosexuals enjoy by virtue of the state [should] be extended to those who grow up different. And that is all." Andrew's new "liberal" gay politics " . . . does not legislate private tolerance, it declares public equality. . . . Our battle is not for political victory but for personal integrity."

Everyone should read Andrew's article for his sharp critique of the contradictions within Right-wing homophobic thought, and for his delicate filleting of what he calls "moderate," know-nothing, blinders-on types like Sam Nunn. Most important, the article is a kind of manifesto for gay conservatism, and as such it deserves scrutiny.

Every manifesto deserves acolytes as well as scrutiny, and "The Politics of Homosexuality" has earned at least one: Bruce Bawer, who appears a year later [June 13, 1994], in last month's *New Republic*, with "The Stonewall Myth: Can the Gay Rights Movement Get Beyond the Politics of Nostalgia?" Bruce, however, is no Andrew. He's cute enough; you can see him looking rueful and contemplative on the cover of his book *A Place at the Table*, though if you've read the book you'll know Bruce doesn't like it when gay men get dishy and bitchy and talk sissy about boys. He thinks it makes us look bad for the straights. Bruce is serious, more serious even than Andrew, as the big open book in the cover photo proclaims: He's read more than half of it! (Lest anyone think I habitually read the *New Republic*, the playwright David Greenspan gave me Andrew's article, and Andrew Kopkind and several others drew my attention to Bruce's.)

Bruce is not only more serious than Andrew, he's more polite, no mean feat; he's so polite I hate to write that he's also much easier to dismiss, but he is. His article is short and sloppy, and he has this habit of creating paper tigers. Take the eponymous "Stonewall Myth," to which "many gay men and lesbians routinely" subscribe. According to Bruce, these "many" believe gay history started with Stonewall, and regard the riot as "a sacred event that lies beyond the reach of objective discourse." Huh? I don't know anyone who believes that, and I've never encountered such a ridiculous assertion in any work of gay criticism or reportage or even fiction. But Bruce goes on for pages tilting at this windmill and the "politics of nostalgia" that accompanies it. He's also, and I mean this politely, a little slow. It took him five years to figure out that maybe a gay man shouldn't be writing movie reviews for the viciously homophobic *American Spectator*. In his book he is anguished: "Had I been wrong to write for so reactionary a publication? If so, then how did one figure out where to draw the line? Should I refuse to write for the *Nation* because its editors frequently appeared to be apologists for Communism? . . . " etc.

In the article Bruce decides that our real problem is a fear of acceptance, fear of success, a "deep unarticulated fear of that metaphorical place at the table," and so we march in front of TV cameras in our underwear, confirming for all the world that we really *are* sick. (Clothes, worn and discarded, are always bothering Bruce, spandex and leather gear and business suits and bras, his writing is littered with the stuff.) I'll focus mostly on Andrew's meatier, seminal (sigh!) text. (For a polite but mostly thorough reaming of *A Place at the Table*, read David Bergman in the Spring '94 issue of the *Harvard Gay and Lesbian Review*.)

In "The Politics of Homosexuality," Andrew concedes quite a lot of good will to those farthest to the Right. He draws an odd distinction between the "visceral recoil" of bigots and the more cautious discomfort of those homophobes who "sincerely believe" in "discouraging homosexuality," who couch their sincere beliefs in "Thomist argument," in "the natural law tradition, which, for all its failings is a resilient pillar of Western thought." Bigotry, too, is a resilient pillar of Western thought, or it was the last time I checked. Andrew realizes that bigotry "expresses itself in thuggery and name-calling. But there are some [conservatives] who don't support anti-gay violence . . . " Like who, for instance? George Will, Bill Buckley and Cardinal O'Connor have all made token clucking noises about fag-bashing, but the incommensurability of these faint protests with the frightening extent of anti-lesbian and gay violence, which has certainly been encouraged by the very vocal homophobia of "conservatives," might force one to question the sincerity of their admonitions and, further, to question the value of distinguishing "Thomist" homophobes from the "thugs" who in 1993 attacked or killed more than 1,900 lesbians and gay men (at least these are the hate crimes we know about).

Andrew takes a placid view of people on the reactionary Right because he is convinced their days are numbered. But does he really believe that Pat Buchanan is now "reduced to joke-telling"? Such a conclusion is possible only if one ignores the impressive, even terrifying political energies of the religious Right. Since Andrew decides political discourse can only countenance "reason and restraint," he of course must exclude the bible-thumpers, who are crazy and *loud*. But the spectrum is more crowded, and on the Right less well-behaved than a gentleman like Andrew cares to admit. His is an endearing reticence, but it is not wise.

Andrew is at his best describing the sorts of traumas homophobia inflicts on its victims (though to nobody's surprise he doesn't care for the word "victim"), yet he's quick to give up on the antidiscrimination legislation of those he calls liberals. "However effective or comprehensive antidiscrimination laws are, they cannot reach far enough." They can't give us confidence, and they only "scratch the privileged surface." "As with other civil rights legislation, those least in need of it may take fullest advantage: the most litigious and articulate homosexuals, who would likely brave the harsh winds of homophobia in any case."

It's unclear whether or not Andrew opposes such legislation which, it seems to me, is worthwhile even if it is only moderately effective. I assume that in limiting the gay rights movement's ambitions to fighting "proactive" discrimination, he is arguing against trying to pass laws that regulate "reactive" discrimination, though I can't find anything in his very specific article that states this opposition specifically or definitively. (In any case, his distinction between *reactive* and *proactive* discrimination falls apart as soon as one considers adoption laws or education or sexual harassment.) Perhaps he's vague because he knows he hasn't much of a case. What worries him especially is that the Right will make effective propaganda out of the argument that "civil rights laws essentially dictate the behavior of heterosexuals, in curtailing their ability to discriminate." And he argues further that this argument "contains a germ of truth."

The argument is unquestionably good propaganda for homophobes, but it's identical to the NRA's argument for giving every nutbag in the country access to a semi-automatic. (Don't curtail their ability to be armed nutbags!) We have to argue such propaganda down, not run away from the legislation that inspires it. As for the "germ of truth," Andrew writes: "Before most homosexuals come out of the closet they are demanding concessions from the majority, a clear curtailment of economic and social liberties, in order to ensure protections few of them will even avail themselves of. It is no wonder there is opposition."

This is a very peculiar view of the processes by which enfranchisement is extended: Civil rights, apparently, are not rights at all, not something inalienable, to which one is entitled by virtue of being human or a citizen, but concessions the majority makes to a minority if and only if the minority can promise it will *use* those rights. Antidiscrimination laws are seen as irrelevant to creating a safer environment in which closeted or otherwise-oppressed people might feel more free to exercise their equality; laws apparently cannot *encourage* freedom, only punish transgressions against it.

The argument that antidiscrimination laws violate "majority" freedoms can be and has been used to eliminate the basis of most of the legislation from the civil rights movement. Affirmative action, housing and employment laws, and voter redistricting can all be said to curtail the freedom of bigots to discriminate, which is in fact what such measures are supposed to do. The connection that such legislation implies between gay rights and other minority rights displeases Andrew, who resists the idea that, as forms of oppressions, homophobia and racism have much in common.

With homosexuality, according to Andrew, "the option of self-concealment has always existed," something that cannot be said about race. (I could introduce him to some flaming creatures who might make him question that assessment, but never mind.) "Gay people are not uniformly discriminated against, *openly* gay people are." Certainly there are important differences of kind and degree and consequence between racism and homophobia, but the idea that invisibility exempts anyone from discrimination is perverse. To need to be invisible, or to feel that you need to be, if there is reason for that fear, is to be discriminated against. The fact that homophobia differs significantly from racism—and loathe as I am to enter the discrimination olympics, I would argue that the consequences of racism in America today are worse than those of homophobia—does not mean that people engaged in one struggle can't learn or borrow from another, or that the tools one oppressed people have developed can't be used to try to liberate others.

Andrew is joined by Bruce in his anxiety to preserve the differences among various kinds of oppression, but they both seem less interested in according each group its own "integrity," as Andrew rightly calls it, than in preventing gay rights from being shanghaied by the radical Left. "The standard post-Stonewall practice . . . indiscriminately link[s] the movement for gay equal rights with any Left-wing cause to which any gay leader might happen to have a personal allegiance" (this is from Bruce's article). "Such linkages have been a disaster for the gay rights movement: Not only do they imply that most gay people sympathize with those so-called progressive movements, but they also serve to reinforce the idea of homosexuality itself as a 'progressive' phenomenon, as something essentially political in nature." Andrew meanwhile warns against the "universalist temptation," which exercises "an enervating and dissipating effect on gay radicalism's political punch."

Gay radicalism's political punch is not something either Andrew or Bruce wishes to see strengthened. Conservative gay politics is in a sense the politics of containment: Connections made with a broadly defined Left are what must be contained. The pair predicts the emergence of increasing numbers of conservative homosexuals (presumably white—in both Andrew's and Bruce's prophecies they come from the suburbs), who are unsympathetic to the idea of linking their fortunes with any other political cause. The future depends not on collectivity and solidarity, but on homosexual individualism—on lesbians and gay men instructing the straight world quietly, "person by person, life by life, heart by heart" (Andrew); to "do the hard, painstaking work of *getting* straight America used to it" (Bruce).

Like all assimilationists, Andrew and Bruce are unwilling to admit that structural or even particularly formidable barriers exist between themselves and their straight oppressors. And for all their elaborate fears that misbehaving queers alienate instead of communicate, there is nowhere in these articles a concern that people of color or the working class or the poor are not being communed with. The audience we are ostensibly losing is identified exclusively as phobic straights, "families" (which one suspects are two-parent, middle class) and gay teenagers.

Bruce and Andrew are very concerned about young gay people. Watching a "lean and handsome" fifteen year old leaf through the *New York Native* at the start of his book, Bruce worries that queer radicalism, sexual explicitness and kink frighten gay kids and the families from whence they come. Probably it is the case that teenagers are freaked by photo ads for The Dungeon. But the *Native* is not produced for teenagers. Images of adult lesbian and gay desire can't be tailored to appeal to fifteen year olds and their straight parents. Our culture is the manifest content of our lives, not a carefully constructed recruiting brochure. True, there aren't readily available, widely circulated images of homosexual domesticity or accomplishment or happiness, but I'd be more inclined to blame the homophobic media than gay radicalism for that. Nor does the need for such images mandate the abandonment of public declarations of and *for* the variety of sexual desire, the public denial and repression of which is after all The Problem. Lesbian and gay kids will have less trouble accepting their homosexuality not when the Gay Pride Parade is an orderly procession of suits arranged in monogamous pairs but when people learn to be less horrified by sex and its complexities.

Out of the great stew of class, race, gender and sexual politics that inspirits the contentious, multiplying, endlessly unfixed lesbian and gay community in America, gay conservatism manages to pick out a majority who are virtually indistinguishable in behavior and aspirations and *Weltanschauung* from the straight world, and a minority of deviants and malcontents who are fucking things up for everyone, thwarting the only realizable goal, which is normalcy.

Andrew says up front that politics is supposed to relieve anxiety. I'd say that it's supposed to relieve misery and injustice. When all that can be expected from politics, in the way of immediate or even proximate social transformation, are gay weddings and gay platoons, the vast rest of it all, every other agony inflicted by homophobia, will have to be taken care of by some cultural osmotic process of quiet individualized persuasion, which will take many many many years. It's the no-government approach to social change. You can hear it argued now against school desegregation, or any attempt to guarantee equal education; you can hear it argued against welfare or job programs. It's the legacy of trickle-down, according to which society should change slowly, organically, spontaneously, without interference, an approach that requires not so much the "discipline, commitment, responsibility" that Bruce exhorts us to—we already practice those—but a great appalling luxury of time (which maybe the editor of the *New Republic* and the erstwhile movie critic of the *American Spectator* can afford), after the passage of which many many many more miserable lives will have been spent or dispensed with. I am always suspicious of the glacier-paced patience of the Right.

Such a politics of homosexuality is dispiriting. Like conservative thought in general, it offers very little in the way of hope, and very little in the way of vision. We shall soon have gay GIs and same-sex confectionery couples atop wedding cakes. This is important, but it's not enough. I expect both hope and vision from my politics. Andrew and Bruce offer nothing more than that gay culture will dissolve invisibly into straight culture, all important difference elided.

I think both Andrew and Bruce would call this assessment unfair. Andrew's politics may be roomier than Bruce's; Andrew is more worldly and generous (except, apparently, when it comes to the theater). Both men have a vision. They see before them an attainable civic peace, in which gay men and lesbians live free of fear (of homophobia, at least), in which gay kids aren't made to feel worthless, or worse, because they're gay.

But what of all the other things gay men and lesbians have to fear? What of the things gay children have to fear, in common with all children? What of the planetary despoilment that kills us? Or the financial necessity that drives some of us into unsafe, insecure, stupid, demeaning and ill-paying jobs? Or the unemployment that impoverishes some of us? Or the racism some of us face? Or the rape some of us fear? What about AIDS? Is it enough to say: Not our problem? Of course gay and lesbian politics is a progressive politics: It depends on progress for the accomplishment of any of its goals. Is there any progressive politics that recognizes no connectedness, no border crossings, no solidarity or possibility for mutual aid?

"A map of the world that does not include Utopia is not worth even glancing at, for it leaves out the one country at which Humanity is always landing." This is neither Bruce nor Andrew, but that most glorious and silly gay writer, Oscar Wilde. Because this is the twenty-fifth anniversary of Stonewall, that mythic moment that lies beyond all objective discourse (just kidding, Bruce!), we are all thinking big. That's what anniversaries are for, to invite consideration of the past and contemplation of the future. And so, to lift my sights and spirits after the dour, pinched anti-politics of gay conservatism, I revisited Oscar, a *lavish* thinker, as he appears in political drag in his magnificent essay, "The Soul of Man Under Socialism."

Oscar, like our two boys, was an individualist, though rather more individual in the way he lived, and much less eager to conform. It would be stretching things to say Oscar was a radical, exactly, though if Bruce and Andrew had been his contemporaries, Lord knows how they would have tut-tutted at his scandalous carryings-on.

Oscar's socialism is an exaltation of the individual, of the individual's immense capacities for beauty and for pleasure. Behind Oscar's socialist politics, wrote John Cowper Powys, is "a grave Mirandola-like desire to reconcile the woods of Arcady with the Mount of Transfiguration." What could be swoonier? Or, with all due deference to Andrew and Bruce's *sober, rational* politics of homosexuality, what could be more gay?

Powys also wrote that Oscar's complaint against capitalism and industrialism is "the irritation of an extremely sensitive *skin* [emphasis added] . . . combined with a pleasure-lover's annoyance at seeing other people so miserably wretched." If there is a relationship between socialism and homosexual liberation, perhaps this is it: an irritation of the skin.

"One's regret," Oscar tells us, "is that society should be constructed on such a basis that man is forced into a groove in which he cannot freely develop what is wonderful and fascinating and delightful in him—in which, in fact, he misses the true pleasure and joy of living." Socialism, as an alternative to individualism politically and capitalism economically, must surely have as its ultimate objective the restitution of the joy of living we may have lost when we first picked up a tool. Towards what other objective is it worthy to strive?

Perhaps the far horizon of lesbian and gay politics is a socialism of the skin. Our task is to confront the political problematics of desire and repression. As much as Bruce and Andrew want to distance themselves from the fact, Stonewall was a sixties thing, part of the utopian project of that time (and the sixties, Joan Nestle writes, is "the favorite target of people who take delight in the failure of dreams"). Honoring the true desire of the skin, and the connection between the skin and heart and mind and soul, is what homosexual liberation is about.

Gay rights may be obtainable, on however broad or limited a basis, but liberation depends on a politics that goes beyond, not an anti-politics. Our unhappiness as scared queer children doesn't only isolate us, it also politicizes us. It inculcates in us a desire for connection that is all the stronger because we have experienced its absence. Our suffering teaches us solidarity; or it should.

This essay was first published in the July 4, 1994 issue of the Nation.

WITH A LITTLE HELP
FROM MY FRIENDS

Angels in America, Parts One and Two, has taken five years to write, and as the work nears completion I find myself thinking a great deal about the people who have left their traces in these texts. The fiction that artistic labor happens in isolation, and that artistic accomplishment is exclusively the provenance of individual talents, is politically charged and, in my case at least, repudiated by the facts.

While the primary labor on *Angels* has been mine, over two dozen people have contributed words, ideas and structures to these plays: actors, directors, audiences, one-night stands, my former lover and many friends. Two in particular, my closest friend, Kimberly T. Flynn (*Perestroika* is dedicated to her), and the man who commissioned *Angels* and helped shape it, Oskar Eustis, have had profound, decisive influences. Had I written these plays without the participation of my collaborators, they would be entirely different—would, in fact, never have come to be.

Americans pay high prices for maintaining the myth of the Individual: We have no system of universal health care, we don't educate our children, we can't pass sane gun control laws, we elect presidents like Reagan, we hate and fear inevitable processes like aging and death. Way down close to the bottom of the list of the evils Individualism visits on our culture is the fact that in the modern era it isn't enough to write; you must also be a Writer, and play your part as the protagonist in a cautionary narrative in which you will fail or triumph, be in or out, hot or cold. The rewards can be fantastic; the punishment dismal; it's a zero sum game, and its guarantor of value, its marker is that you pretend you play it solo, preserving the myth that you alone are the wellspring of your creativity.

When I started to write these plays, I wanted to attempt something of ambition and size even if that meant I might be accused of straying too close to ambition's ugly twin, pretentiousness. Given the bloody opulence of this country's great and terrible history, given its newness and its grand improbability, its artists are bound to be tempted towards large gestures and big embraces, a proclivity de Tocqueville deplored as a national artistic trait nearly two hundred years ago. Melville, my favorite American writer, strikes inflated, even hysterical, chords on occasion. It's the sound of the Individual ballooning, overreaching. We are all children of "Song of Myself." And maybe in this spacious, under- and depopulated, as yet only lightly inscribed country, the Individual will finally expand to its unstable, insupportably swollen limits, and pop. (But here I risk pretentiousness, and an excess of optimism to boot—another American trait.)

Anyone interested in exploring alternatives to Individualism and the political economy it serves, Capitalism, has to be willing to ask hard questions about the ego, both as abstraction and as exemplified in oneself.

Bertolt Brecht, while he was still in Weimar-era Berlin and facing the possibility of participating in a socialist revolution, wrote a series of remarkable short plays, his *Lehrstücke*, or learning plays. The principal subject of these plays was the painful dismantling, as a revolutionary necessity, of the individual ego. This dismantling is often figured, in the learning plays, as death.

Brecht, who never tried to hide the dimensions of his own titanic personality, didn't sentimentalize the problems such personalities present, or the process of loss involved in letting go of the richness, and the riches, that accompany successful self-creation.

Brecht simultaneously claimed and mocked the identity he'd won for himself, "a great German writer," raising important questions about the means of literary production, challenging the sacrosanctity of the image of the solitary artist and, at the same time, openly, ardently wanting to be recognized as a genius. That he was a genius is inarguably the case. For a man deeply committed to collectivity as an ideal and an achievable political goal, this blazing singularity was a mixed blessing at best and at worst, an obstacle to a blending of radical theory and practice.

In the lower right-hand corner of the title page of many of Brecht's plays you will find, in tiny print, a list of names under the heading "collaborators." Sometimes these people contributed little, sometimes a great deal. One cannot help feeling that those who bore those minuscule names, who expended the considerable labor the diminutive typography conceals, have gotten a bum deal. Many of these effaced collaborators, Ruth Berlau, Elisabeth Hauptmann, Margarete Steffin, were women. In the question of shared intellectual and artistic labor, gender is always an issue.

On the day last spring when the Tony nominations were being handed out [May 1993], I left the clamorous room at Sardi's thinking gloomily that here was another source of anxiety, another obstacle to getting back to work rewriting *Perestroika*. In the building's lobby I was introduced to the producer Elizabeth I. McCann, who said to me: "I've been worried about how you were handling all this, till I read that you have an Irish woman in your life. Then I knew you were going to be fine." Ms. McCann was referring to Kimberly T. Flynn; an article in the *New Yorker* last year about *Angels in America* described how certain features of our shared experience dealing with her prolonged health crisis, caused by a serious cab accident several years ago, had a major impact on the plays.

Kimberly and I share Louisiana childhoods (she's from New Orleans, I grew up in Lake Charles); different but equally complicated, powerful religious traditions and an ambivalence towards those traditions; Left politics informed by liberation struggles (she as a feminist, I as a gay man), as well as socialist and psychoanalytic theory; and a belief in the effectiveness of activism and the possibility of progress.

From the beginning Kimberly was my teacher. Though largely self-taught, she was more widely read and she helped me understand both Freud and Marx. She introduced me to the writers of the Frankfurt School and their early attempts at synthesizing psychoanalysis and Marxism; and to the German philosopher and critic Walter Benjamin, whose importance for me rests primarily in his introduction into these "scientific" disciplines a Kabbalist-inflected mysticism and a dark, apocalyptic spirituality.

As both writer and talker Kimberly employs a rich variety of rhetorical strategies and effects, even while expressing deep emotion. She identifies this as an Irish trait; it's evident in O'Neill, Yeats, Beckett. This relationship to language, blended with Jewish and gay versions of the same strategies, is evident in my plays, in the ways my characters speak.

More pessimistic than I, Kimberly is much less afraid to look at the ugliness of the world. She tries to protect herself far less than I do, and consequently she sees more. She feels safest, she says, knowing the worst, while most people I know, myself included, would rather be spared and feel safer encircled by a measure of obliviousness. She's capable of pulling things apart, teasing out fundamental concerns from their camouflage; at the same time she uses her analysis, her learning, her emotions, her lived experience, to make imaginative leaps, to see the deeper connections between ideas and historical developments. Through her example I learned to trust that such leaps can be made; I learned to admire them, in literature, in theory, in the utterances people make in newspapers. And certainly it was in part her example that made the labor of synthesizing disparate, seemingly unconnected things become for me the process of writing a play.

Since the accident Kimberly has struggled with her health, and I have struggled to help her, sometimes succeeding, sometimes failing; and it doesn't take much more than a passing familiarity with *Angels* to see how my life and my plays match up. It's always been easier talking about the way in which I used what we've lived through to write *Angels*, even though I sometimes question the morality of the act (while at the same time considering it unavoidable if I was to write at all), than it has been acknowledging the intellectual debt. People seem to be more interested in the story of the accident and its aftermath than in the intellectual genealogy, the emotional life being privileged over the intellectual life in the business of making plays, and the two being regarded, incorrectly, as separable. A great deal of what I understand about health issues comes from what Kimberly has endured and triumphed over, and the ways she's articulated those experiences. But *Angels* is more the result of our intellectual friendship than it is autobiography. Her contribution was as contributor, teacher, editor, adviser, not muse.

Perhaps other playwrights don't have similar relationships or similar debts; perhaps they have. In a wonderful, recently published collection of essays on creative partnerships, entitled *Significant Others*, edited by Isabelle de Courtivron and Whitney Chadwick, the contributors examine both healthy and deeply unhealthy versions of artistic interdependence in such couples as the Delaunays, Kahlo and Rivera, Hammett and Hellman, and Jasper Johns and Robert Rauschenberg—and in doing so strike forcefully at what the editors call "the myth of solitariness."

We have no words for the people to whom we are indebted. I call Oskar Eustis a dramaturg, sometimes a collaborator; but collaborator implies co-authorship and nobody knows what "dramaturg" implies. *Angels*, I wrote in the published version of *Perestroika*, began in a conversation, real and imaginary, with Oskar Eustis. A romantic-ambivalent love for American history and belief in what one of the play's characters calls "the prospect of some sort of radical democracy spreading outward and growing up" are things Oskar and I share, part of the discussions we had for nearly a year before I started writing *Millennium*. Oskar continues to be for me, intellectually and emotionally, what the developmental psychologists call "a secure base of attachment" (a phrase I learned from Kimberly).

The play is indebted, too, to writers I've never met. It's ironical that Harold Bloom, in his introduction to Olivier Revault d'Allonnes' *Musical Variations on Jewish Thought*, provided me with a translation of the Hebrew word for "blessing"—"more life"—which subsequently became key to the heart of *Perestroika*. Harold Bloom is also the author of *The Anxiety of Influence*, his oedipalization of the history of Western literature, which when I first encountered it years ago made me so anxious my analyst suggested I put it away. Recently I had the chance to meet Professor Bloom and, guilty over my appropriation of "more life," I fled from the encounter as one of Freud's *Totem and Taboo* tribesmen might flee from a meeting with that primal father, the one with the big knife. (I cite Bloom as the source of the idea in the published script.)

Guilt plays a part in this confessional account; and I want the people who helped me make this play to be identified, because their labor was consequential. I have been blessed with remarkable comrades and collaborators: Together we organize the world for ourselves, or at least we organize our understanding of it; we reflect it, refract it, criticize it, grieve over its savagery and help each other to discern, amidst the gathering dark, paths of resistance, pockets of peace and places from whence hope may be plausibly expected. Marx was right: The smallest indivisible human unit is two people, not one; one is a fiction. From such nets of souls societies, the social world, human life springs. And also plays.

This essay was first published in the New York Times *on November 21, 1993, and later appeared as the "Afterword" to* Angels in America, Part Two: Perestroika, *February 1994.*

SOME QUESTIONS
ABOUT TOLERANCE

Presented at the "Tolerance as an Art Form" conference,
New York City, February 9, 1993.

I wanted to participate in this conference because bigotry of every kind seems these days to be getting an upper hand. I don't know whether or not we are witnessing a massive regression in the face of economic and social disorganization, or the turbulence that invariably accompanies a transformation—the last ugly efforts of reactionary forces worldwide to prevent an imminent and unstoppable outbreak of sanity and peace. Not all signs are negative these days, but there's much cause for alarm.

Only once I'd agreed to participate I became completely confused and conflicted about what I wanted to say. I've finally located my conflict and rendered it in the form of a kind of dissenting opinion. I worry that I haven't fulfilled my assignment. I'm sure I can count on being tolerated.

The title of this conference uses two words I don't trust: "Tolerance" and "Art."

If Equality is the chief civic virtue of liberal democracy, and Fraternity and Sorority the chief virtues of socialist democracy, then Tolerance, to borrow from Robert Wolff, is the chief virtue of a pluralist democracy, which is the best description of and possibly the best prescription for the kind of society the United States is and ought to be. In a large, industrialized pluralist democracy, groups of people, arranged along lines of race, ethnicity, religion, gender and sexual orientation, must develop strategies for living together in spite of what may prove to be incommensurable differences. The art of doing this is called Tolerance. Or so the theory goes.

Tolerance has its uses, but not all of them are good. It seems to me that frequently when people are asked to tolerate one another, something is wrong that Tolerance will not fix. Tolerance as a virtue derives from the humanist notion that we are all, as the old saying goes, brothers under the skin; and in this bland, unobjectionable assertion is much that can be objected to. We are divided not simply by "intolerance" but by brutal discrepancies in wealth and power; the qualities that distinguish us from each other are not simply surface irrelevancies but our histories and cultures; and we aren't all "brothers."

When we hear the word "intolerance" in the context of contemporary events we think of Crown Heights; the Los Angeles uprisings; the rape of Moslem women in Bosnia; gay-bashing; born-again anti-Semitism in Germany and here at home. These are events too various to be grouped under one rubric, and any word broad enough to seem to encompass so much should immediately arouse our suspicions.

Intolerance implies a passive, xenophobic bridling at foreignness, while the various phenomena that have impelled us to assemble here today are far more active, passionate and exuberantly malevolent than that. In other countries, where it is polite to use the word, the agents of what we are calling intolerance are called fascists. And Tolerance is not an adequate response to fascism.

Tolerance can be used to normalize an insupportable situation, or it can serve to warn those groups which lack real power that they exist on sufferance, that they are tolerated. If you are oppressed, if those characteristics which make you identifiable to yourself make you loathsome to a powerful majority which does not share those characteristics, then you are at great risk if your existence is predicated on being tolerated. Toleration is necessary when power is unequal; if you have power, you will not need to be tolerated. People who are oppressed need to strive for power, which in a pluralistic democracy means they have to strive for civil rights, for legal protection, for enfranchisement. Ineffable benevolences like Tolerance are easily and tracelessly withdrawn. Civic peace is most secure when the law guarantees it. In other words, people seeking to rid their society of racism, homophobia, anti-Semitism and misogyny must engage in political struggles.

The dismaying lack of solidarity for the oppressed by the oppressed is historically at its worst when the Right is most successful. This, too, is a political issue.

There is a false notion that Culture unites people and Politics divides them. I believe this to be untrue. Every people, every group has a culture, but each culture is different; the artistic expressions of each culture embody those differences in form and content, and indeed one might say that the art a culture produces is the clearest statement that culture can make of difference. While we may say, hopefully, that no difference is insuperable, the recognition and embracing of difference, rather than its

effacement, is what real integration and real multicultur-
alism mandate. We do not want to be overhasty in seeking out unity in culture. We understand very little about
the processes by which different cultures may engage
constructively with one another, for our history is a history of cultural murder, genocide, holocaust, ethnic cleansing—our history is the history of the violent eradication
of Otherness. Where we have succeeded in striking bal-
ances which allow for the possibility of mutual coexistence, we have relied on politics as the instrument of
peace.

How much sense does it make to separate Culture and
Politics as distinct categories? If culture can be thought
of as both the exalted and the quotidian expressions of a
people's life, then all culture is ideological, political, root-
ed in history and informed by present circumstance. And
art has to reflect this, as well as reflect the artist's desires
for society and social change which will, whether revolutionary or reactionary, find expression in the work he or
she creates.

If art (and here I lapse into the sin of being generic,
though it is really the art of the theater I know and am
speaking about) has any political impact, and I believe it
does, it seems to me that it's most likely to have it by
being effective as art—in other words, that political agendas can't successfully be imposed on the act of making
art, of creation, for all that those agendas will invariably
surface from within once the art is made.

The artist embraces or expresses difference, spends her
or his time imagining it with as powerful and graceful
empathic leaps as the limitations of human consciousness permit. This embrace of difference can be instruc-

tive: The artist is involved in a process of synthesis when imagining the Other—synthesis, and not compromise. As in any process of true synthesis, the two principles, the Self and the Other, create something new without losing those features which make each principle distinctly itself. This process is difficult and doomed to at least partial failure—if the Other is to stay truly Other then failure is axiomatic. But when an audience watches an artist in this process it is exhilarated, because a miracle of sorts is taking place, in which the Self's isolation is being discarded but not at the cost of its integrity. It is in moments like these, when art is most successful, that it may perhaps teach useful gestures to society, to political action.

I do not believe that a lack of exposure to other cultures in and of itself breeds the virulent forms of hatred that lead to violence. Nor does exposure guarantee Tolerance. In the communities of what was formerly Yugoslavia, different cultures living in the greatest intimacy possible, including intermarriage, integrated schools and housing, have split into stark factions, and the Serbs are now massacring Bosnian Moslems who were formerly next-door neighbors.

Neither cultural intimacy nor art can ensure coexistence, not when politics makes faction profitable, or seem so. I would like it to be the case, for instance, that New York City schoolboard homophobe Mary Cummins or John J. O'Connor watch one of my plays and subsequently abandon their energetic persecution of gay men and women. I think it unlikely that they will buy tickets, much less be moved to decency by art, when the manifest suffering of people around them has not moved them at all. Perhaps there is more hope for less grimly committed ideologues; but the homophobic rage on display during the battle over the Children of the Rainbow curriculum does not seem to me to be of the sort that will yield to theater. The failure of that initiative is a useful example of the ways in which mistakes in the political arena led to a firestorm of hysterical intolerance, and much worse. The remedy, I believe, lies not in cultural exchange, an unmediated example of which could be seen at those nightmare Board of Education meetings, where the Legions of Decency screeched their opposition into silence, but in politics.

New York City drew me from my native Louisiana seventeen years ago because I imagined it a place in which people of fantastically varied backgrounds could live, intimately, intricately mixed. When I first arrived, every subway car seemed to me a peaceable kingdom in miniature, in which Difference charged the air with curiosity, mystery, possibility and sex. As a gay man, I desperately wanted to believe that such a city existed, and even if New York never really was such a place, in the early seventies it still appeared to be headed towards a reasonable approximation. Twelve years of the anti-urban initiatives of the Reagan and Bush administrations, of polarizing and hate-mongering leaders like Ed Koch, of increased homelessness and joblessness and decreased funding for health care, education and social services have changed this city. The hope offered by the identity-politics movements has collided catastrophically with the counterrevolution, and the temporary deferral of that hope has given birth to frustration and desperation; which in turn has given birth to a politics based on nationalism. Nationalism, however useful it might prove to be in weathering a hostile social environment, brings with it moral blindness and heavily defended, bristling boundaries. Our best hope, I believe, for reclaiming lost ground and for pushing ahead lies not so much in cultural exchange but in securing civil rights. Before we can lay claim to our common humanity, we must learn to recognize and respect Difference and what it tells us about the infinite complexities of human behavior—recognize and respect Difference, not just tolerate it. The foregrounding of such respect is social justice.

This essay was first published by the National Assembly of Local Arts Agencies in the May/June 1993 issue of Monographs.

COPIOUS, GIGANTIC, AND SANE

Presented on the occasion of the March on Washington
for Gay and Lesbian Rights, April 25, 1993.

The first time I had sex with a man, I was twenty-one years old and afterwards I had a nightmare. I was lying with my lover in a strange bed, and he was asleep. I was visited by the ghost of the African-American man who for decades had worked as the foreman at my family's lumber company in Louisiana. His name was Rufus Berard, and I'd adored him when I was a child; he had died when I was still very young. In my nightmare he was looking at me lying on rumpled sheets alongside the man with whom I'd just spent a wonderful carnal evening. Rufus was staring not unkindly, but with unsettling intensity, refusing to speak and weeping silently.

Then my paternal grandfather arrived. He looked ill (which at the time of the dream he was) and angry (which he seldom was), a cancer-ridden Jeremiah. He had come to pronounce anathema: "You're going to die," he said with immense loathing and satisfaction, this man who had always been a loving grandparent. "There's something wrong in your bones." And having handed down my death sentence, he walked away, back into the Cave of the Psyche, home to goblins.

Rufus, continuing to cry, watched my grandfather go. Before vanishing into deep-indigo shadows, my grandfather turned back to me. As if in answer to a question I'd asked about Rufus's silent, mournful presence in the dream, my grandfather said, "He's the Black Other," and disappeared. Rufus smiled at me and I woke up.

I've forgotten certain details about the first man I slept with, whom I did not see again, but the bleak and dire vision our happy sex conjured up remains with me, as vivid as any recollected actual experience. When AIDS first became an inescapable feature on the landscape, the dream came back to me often in broad daylight: Learning that a friend was sick or seropositive, waiting for my own test results, my dream-grandfather's words would frighten me with what seemed an awful premonitory power.

But in this nocturnal drama of guilt and patriarchal damnation, my unconscious also saw fit to write a character bearing not only compassion but kinship, and a way out of death into life and life's political, social concomitant: liberation.

I grew up in a small southern city in the sixties, in the culture of "genteel" post-integration bayou-country racism. The African-American population of Lake Charles, Louisiana was ghettoized and impoverished; black women, referred to by their employers as "girls" even though many were middle-aged or older, entered the homes of white people through years, lifetimes of domestic servitude, and black men performed the poorly remunerated labor white men wouldn't do. There were countless incidents of discrimination and occasionally bias crimes, but southern Louisiana wasn't at that time Klan country—David Duke is a recent blight, the ugly and publicly disinherited spawn of Reagan and Bush and Lee Atwater. I remember a certain white civic pride that in Lake Charles racism was (theoretically at least) tempered by a spirit of cooperation and mutual avoidance, and brutality wasn't something decent people engaged in, even in the name of preserving white supremacy. And yet of course anyone black in my hometown was like anyone black anywhere in the United States: feared, subjected to indignity and abuse, dehumanized, Other as Americans understand and have historically responded to the Other—as a negation of good, as Death, as ripe for extermination.

Part of me understood the phantasm of the grieving black man who visited me that night as a figure of my own demise. But his presence had a doubleness that is important to consider. Toni Morrison, in *Playing in the Dark*, writes: "Images of blackness can be evil *and* protective, rebellious *and* forgiving, fearful *and* desirable—all the self-contradictory features of the self."

One of my most vivid memories from childhood is from the day of Martin Luther King's funeral. I watched it on TV with Maudi Lee Davis, the woman who worked as my family's maid. Maudi cried throughout the broadcast, and I was both frightened and impressed—I felt her powerful grief connected us, her and me and my quiet hometown, with the struggle I knew was being waged in the world, in history. It was an instant in which one feels that one is being changed as the world is changed, and I believe I was.

I don't know what power it is in human beings that keeps us going against indescribable forces of destruction. I don't know how any African-American, any person of color in this country stays sane, given that the whole machinery of American racism seems designed to drive them crazy or kill them. I don't know why it is every woman isn't completely consumed all the time by debilitating rage. I don't know why lesbians and gay men aren't all as twisted and wrecked inside as Roy Cohn was. By means of what magic do people transform bitter centuries of enslavement and murder into Beauty and Grace? One mustn't take these miracles of perseverance for granted, nor rejoice in them too much, forgetting the oceans of spilled blood of all the millions who didn't make it, who succumbed. But something, some joy in us, refuses death, makes us stand against the overt and insidious violence practiced upon us by death's minions.

Something in me, smarter than me, pointed the way towards identification with the Black Other, towards an embrace of my status as a pariah, as rejected, as a marginal man. I learned, we learn, to transform the gestures, postures and etiquette of oppression into an identity; we learn to take what history has made of us and claim it proudly as what we are, and choose to be. We refuse victim status, we constitute ourselves as history's agents rather than as its accidents, and even if that's only partly true, such a claim empowers us, and makes us grow too big for shackles, for kitchens, for closets, for ghettos of all kinds. Wayne Koestenbaum, in his brilliant book, *The Queen's Throat*, writes: "One is fixed in a class, a race, a gender. But against such absolutes there arises a fervent belief in *retaliatory self invention* [emphasis added] . . . to help the stigmatized self imagine it is received, believed, and adored." We find love, in other words, that Great Ineffable that breaks through our hermetically sealed worlds of private pain and disgrace and self-hatred, that unites us with others, that makes us willing to give up even life itself for more connection, more strength, more love.

I grew up hating being gay, hating not only myself but those like me, so much so that in college I evinced such a deep disdain for homosexuality that I repulsed the boy with whom I first fell in love. I feel only part of the way out of that miasma, and I am at times awestruck by the staying power and persuasiveness and pervasiveness of shame. I can almost rival Woody Allen for years in thera-py, and I am convinced that as necessary as it is, therapy alone cannot heal the soul. Only community can.

And that's why I am going to Washington on Sunday, to join with at least a million Others who, like me, locate our difference in whom we choose to take to bed. And among that million there are many deep rifts and factions and differences, but we share enough to come together, to announce to those who deprive us of our rights that we will not be silent again, and to heal ourselves by congregating.

Walt Whitman, The Good Gay Poet, wrote in *An American Primer*:

When the time comes for [words] to represent any thing or any state of things, the words will surely follow. The lack of any words, I say again, is as historical as the existence of words. As for me, I feel a hundred realities, clearly determined in me, that words are not yet formed to represent. Men like me—also women, our counterparts, perfectly equal—will gradually get to be more and more numerous—perhaps swiftly, in shoals; then the words will also follow, in shoals.

There aren't words, or I can't find the words, to describe this moment: when the gray forbidding wall of Oppression starts to crack, when a space opens up between the sky and the horizon, when change becomes possible. For all the manifold horrors of the present day—ethnic cleansing, nationalism and fascism recrudescing, the calamity in Waco, and the ongoing decimation of AIDS— I am going to Washington full of hope. The whole city will be as queer as the Castro on a Saturday night— queerer, because there will be gay women there and gays of color and old people and fat people and disabled people and even heterosexuals who are Gay for the Day. We will be a community in the process of transforming itself and the world, the offspring Walt described once in a vision: "Copious, gigantic, and sane."

This essay was first published in the Los Angeles Times *on April 25, 1993.*

ON PRETENTIOUSNESS

The keynote address of the 5th Annual OutWrite Conference,
Boston, March 3, 1995.

Everything I say to you tonight, indeed everything discussed at the conference this weekend, is overshadowed,
if not actually overwhelmed, by the fact that down the
seaboard, in D.C., the scariest congress this country has
ever elected is energetically, industriously, enthusiastical-
ly dismantling the federal government. The America we
live in today, still racked, starved, burned, brutalized and
unrecovered from the pillaging it endured in the eighties,
this present ravaged America will seem in ten years' retro-
spect a paradise; that's an easy prophecy; the future that's
being legislated into existence in these last few weeks is
as we all know no future at all. All the important accom-
plishments of struggle, all the benchmarks of agonizing
progress, are going up in great puffs of unregulated unin-
vestigated nicotine-laden tobacco smoke. In ten years'
time public education through high school will be nothing more than overcrowded indoctrination in Rightist
political cant, supervised by Bill Bennett and his ilk, with
no bad-tasting non-nutritional but at least free lunch.
Affordable public higher education will be virtually
nonexistent. This will help make people even more docile

when faced with downsizing, which surely must produce prodigious rates of unemployment; and there will be no organized labor and no social net. Multinationals will have near-absolute sway over the workplaces and breathing spaces and landscapes and mindscapes and airwaves and informational pathways; corrupt and unaccountable state legislatures will be big business's eager foot-servants; minorities will have no legal protectional guarantees and will be ruthlessly dominated and policed by a pseudo-majority whose real power derives, not from brute numerical superiority, but from an unchallengeable stranglehold on realpolitik financed by multinationals. Progressive taxation will be a memory; the rich will be very rich. Searching police will need no warrants, recent immigrants will have no rights, the rights of the rest of us will go next, civil liberties will be lost, abortion rights will be lost, civil rights legislation will be lost, health care is lost already. Laws that protect children from abuse will be lost. Laws that reinstate death penalties and limit the number of appeals a death-row inmate gets; laws limiting the possibility of suing miscreant corporations, or the government—these will be passed in every state. Guns will be available. Prisons will mushroom. Sodomy laws will mushroom. Public discourse will have degenerated to such abysmal depths George Bush will seem to have been eloquent; there will of course be no federal funding for the arts or humanities. Colleges will offer courses in hokey-scientific theories of race-based genetic superiority, and on the history of the failure of feminism, and though abortion will be illegal, eugenics will be a coming thing. Research on AIDS, research on breast cancer will have stalled; pharmaceutical corporations and managed care corporations and insurance giants will control the medical front, concurrently racking up astronomical profit—the FDA, deeply flawed as it is and has ever been, will be a thing of the past and, dare I say it, missed. Some wizened Republican horror will occupy the White House, and whatever his name is he will be Nixon, he will be Reagan, he will, perhaps in name as well as in spirit, be Newt. You went to bed in 1994, and wake up: It's morning, 1953! Except in 1953 things were better.

And it is no exaggeration to say that as a direct result of the laws and amendments these criminally reckless, criminally stupid, mendacious neo-barbarians are enacting, millions of people will die.

So from underneath this lightless, lengthening, deepening, icy-cold shadow, it's hard to talk about writing. I have even in the best of times only the shakiest faith in art, in the political power of the written word, and in times of political extremity writing seems to me a luxury. It is only because I am in utter helpless thrall to luxury that I continue writing, and reading. We have written a lot, and read a lot, and a lot has been changing, and some of it for the better, and then suddenly you discover that the decisive battle was happening behind you, and though you may have won the skirmish before you, the enemy is swarming up from the rear. And you are fucked. And not pleasantly. Suddenly someone who is the antithesis of what a writer ought to be, someone whose every word is a lie, someone who can't spell "potato" even, has carried the field. So what, my despair asks me at such times, is the use of writing?

The other thing that makes it hard to talk about writing tonight, besides having spent too much time listening, on

C-SPAN, to the Götterdämmerungian Shit-Hits-The-Fan Overture also known as the proceedings of the 104th Congress—the other thing that makes it hard to talk about writing is that this is a roomful of writers I'm talking to; some of you, terrifyingly enough, are very good writers; a few are even great; and I yearn for the moral and aesthetic superiority with which I could protectively enfold myself were I addressing, say, the Heritage Foundation. You *look* fabulous, I admire you I adore you you are my sisters and brothers but you are *writers* and you scare the shit out of me.

The danger I face tonight is that I am back in psychoanalysis and I am in a confessional mood. Forgive me my sins: My problem is fraudulence. As a person who calls himself an artist in the face of the world's determined aggressive downward spiral, I feel a fraud, for this is an era of emergency, of crisis, and art is a self-indulgence; and then when I am among other people who are artists I abandon my ambivalence about *being* an artist and become aware only of how insufficient an artist I am.

For instance: The past two years I've participated in readings in New York City to raise money for the people of Sarajevo. These have, on each occasion, left me depressed—it would be histrionic and rhetorical to say suicidally depressed, but I *am* histrionic and rhetorical and so I say I have felt suicidally depressed. For the reasons mentioned above: In the face of the Bosnian horror, words, art, admirable sentiment, ideas, memory, history, hope—everything fails, or seems to fail. The gap between the words we write and read and the need for action so much greater than any individual has the power to perform—that gap grows too large and I despair. Despair is a sin, I really believe that, but I am as I say a miserable sinner, and there are days after some nights I can't get out of bed. And what made each of those Sarajevo evenings even worse was that my despair and I were surrounded by *writers*, my scrivenophobia excited to its utmost. On both occasions, in fact, I had to sit next to or immediately behind Joseph Brodsky, Big Daddy, the man who told Brezhnev poets always have the last laugh, and he was right. I smiled shyly at Brodsky. He didn't smile back. It took me months to recover.

Last year I dreaded this speech and this conference so much I didn't even show, that's how much I dreaded it. Instead of coming I sent a note of apology, which I believe was read aloud:

October 8, 1993

Dear Michael, Mark and the OutWrite Conference:

Perestroika, Part Two of *Angels in America*, is a play about the difficulties of change, and true to its subject the play and its productions, both here and in London, keep changing in the most difficult ways imaginable. Because of delays in the schedule, the OutWrite Conference falls, not on the second weekend of previews, which was the case when we spoke several months ago, but in the middle of the most arduous and tension-filled technical rehearsals since the Trinity Test at Los Alamos in 1945. Unlike J. Robert Oppenheimer and Company, we are hoping *not* to produce a bomb.

I am as disappointed and sick-at-heart about being a no-show as I was honored to be invited to speak. I feel like the World's Biggest Rat Fink, and I think you should collectively reprove me by hissing as one for fifteen seconds, and then forgive me by praying for me—forgiveness is the secret to maintaining one's youthful looks, and I need the prayers.

And when you're next in New York you should all come to dinner. I'll bake a lasagna.

I'm really really sorry; I send you my deepest apologies, regrets, gratitude for your forbearance, and much much love.

Yours,

Tony Kushner

Even a year later, even now, the fear, the sense of fraudulence, the doubt that I have anything of value to teach anyone, is so great that coherence, as such, is startled out of hiding like game birds from the underbrush, in panicky bursts, and I find I must talk about writing to you writers only obliquely.

So let's talk about lasagna.

Why, my analyst might ask me, did I choose lasagna for last year's palliatory offering? One obvious answer is that it's my favorite among the dishes my mother prepared. I loved it so much that I learned how to do it. I can cook various things now but for a while lasagna was the only thing I could cook and this is how it's made:

Stewed tomatoes, wide flat lasagna noodles, thyme, basil, bay leaves, oregano, black and white pepper, salt, yellow onions, scallions, garlic, green and red peppers, AT LEAST four kinds of cheese: one bland and milky (I prefer cottage cheese to ricotta because the curds have more heft), one white and stinky, one yellow and stinky and one yellow and mellow—AND Parmesan—and beef, fennel pork sausages, olive oil, mushrooms, olives and a deep Pyrex dish. And parsley for the garni.

Lasagna is about opulence. Lasagna should be garlicky garrulous, excessively, even suspiciously generous, promiscuous, flirtatious, insistent, persistent overwhelming exhaustive and exhausting. Perfection in a lasagna I think ought to be measured by the extent to which it effects a balance between fluidity and solidity, between architecture and melting. It is something between a pie and a mélange, there are membranes but they are permeable, the layers must maintain their integrity and yet exist in an exciting dialectic tension to the molten oozy cheesy oily juices which they separate, the goo must almost but not completely successfully threaten the always-discernible-yet-imperiled imposed order.

Baking lasagna has long been my own personal paradigm for writing a play. A good play I think should always feel as though it's only barely been rescued from the brink of chaos, as though all the yummy nutritious ingredients you've thrown into it have almost-but-not-quite succeeded in overwhelming the design. A play should have barely been rescued from the mess it might just as easily have been; just as each slice of lasagna should stand tall, while at the same time betray its entropic desire towards collapse, just as the lasagna should seem to *want* to dissolve into meat and cheese stew, so you can marvel all the more at the culinary engineering magic that holds such entropy at bay, that keeps the unstackable firmly, but not too firmly, stacked. A good play, like a good lasagna, should be overstuffed: It has a pomposity, and an overreach: Its ambitions extend in the direction of not-missing-a-trick, it has a bursting omnipotence up its sleeve, or rather, under its noodles: It is pretentious food.

Pretentiousness, overstatement, rhetoric and histrionics, grandiosity and portentousness are, as much as they are also the tropes of fascists and demagogues everywhere, American tropes, gestures of habitual florid overstep common among those practitioners of American culture to whom I have always been most instantly attracted. It is an aspect of American history and the culture we have developed that I am keen to possess, to transform for my own purposes: the writing of Declarations, Constitutions, Epics, Manifestos. Consider chapter 18 of de Tocqueville's *Democracy in America*, which is entitled "Why American Writers and Speakers Are Often Bombastic," and which is remarkable for its insight, less so for its French anti-democratic snottiness:

> I have often noticed that the Americans, whose language when talking business is clear and dry, without the slightest ornament, and of such extreme simplicity as often to be vulgar, easily turn bombastic when they attempt a poetic style. They are then pompous, without stopping from beginning to end of a speech, and one would have supposed, seeing them thus prodigal of metaphors, that they could never say anything simply.
>
> The reason is easily pointed out.
>
> Each citizen of a democracy generally spends his time considering the interests of a very insignificant person, namely, himself. If he ever does raise his eyes higher, he sees nothing but the huge apparition of society or the even larger form of the human race.

He has nothing between very limited and clear ideas and very general and vague conceptions; the space between is empty. . . .

Writers, for their part, almost always pander to this propensity, which they share; they inflate their imaginations and swell them out beyond bounds, so that they achieve gigantism, missing real grandeur. . . . Writer and public join in corrupting each other. . . . Finding no stuff for the ideal in what is real and true, poets, abandoning truth and reality, create monsters.

I have no fear that the poetry of democratic peoples will be found timid or that it will stick too close to the earth. I am much more afraid that it will spend its whole time getting lost in the clouds and may finish up by describing an entirely fictitious country. I am alarmed at the thought of too many immense, incoherent images, overdrawn descriptions, bizarre effects, and a whole fantastic breed of brainchildren who will make one long for the real world.

So when I began work on *Angels in America*, I felt that the outrageousness of the project I was attempting—offering itself like a fatted calf to critics who loved to feast on pretentiousness and grandiosity—I felt that this selfsame pretentiousness and grandiosity was my birthright as an American, and rather than pointing to some serious deficiencies and flaws in my character—although such deficiencies and flaws undoubtedly exist and are complicit in all of this—my artistic obstreperousness indicated to me, on good days, that I was heir, no matter how puny an heir I might be, to a literary tradition that had produced some of my favorite books.

Chief among which was, and still is, *Moby-Dick*—we know de Tocqueville never met Melville but he might have been describing him in advance. I have always loved the daring, the absurdity, the frequently hair-raising success, and occasional hair-raising failure, the passion and the onrushing grandiloquent devouring recklessness of Melville's writing. It gives me license to try anything.

Melville's first taste of critical disregard came with his book *Mardi*, which is, in my opinion, one of his greatest, clearly a warmup for *Moby-Dick*, which also failed critically. In *Mardi* a fictional Polynesian archipelago, called Mardi, is a stand-in for the entire world. The book begins as a slightly fantasticized version of Melville's early, successful South Sea adventures; but winds of metaphor, the heritage of English literature and contemporary national and international politics soon fill his sails and blow the author, by about a fourth of the way into the book, out of the realm of realism and into a new kind of entirely literary, philosophical, symbol-laden, book-of-a-book—a planet on the table.

The novel is deliriously endless; in chapter 180 we encounter a character who is the Mardian Homer or Virgil or Dante, and his sufferings to produce his masterpiece, an epic called *Koztanza*, are described. But clearly Melville is writing about himself, in a perfectly splendid lament over the high-wire perils, the anxieties suffered by a writer—even a great writer—tilling the vasty fields of pretentiousness:

> Sometimes, when by himself, he thought hugely of [his book] . . . but when abroad, among men, he

almost despised it; but when he bethought him of those parts, written with full eyes, half blinded; temples throbbing; and pain at the heart—He would say to himself, "Sure, it can not be in vain!" Yet again, when he bethought him of the hurry and bustle of Mardi, dejection stole over him. "Who will heed it," thought he; "what care these fops and brawlers for me? But am I not myself an egregious coxcomb? Who will read me? Say one thousand pages—twenty-five lines each—every line ten words—every word ten letters. That's two million five hundred thousand *a*'s, and *i*'s, and *o*'s to read! How many are superfluous? Am I not mad to saddle Mardi with such a task? Of all men, am I the wisest, to stand upon a pedestal, and teach the mob? Ah, my own *Koztanza*! Child of many prayers!—in whose earnest eyes, so fathomless, I see my own; and recall all past delights and silent agonies—thou may'st prove, as the child of some fond dotard: beauteous to me; hideous to Mardi! And methinks, that while so much slaving merits that thou should'st not die; it has not been intense, prolonged enough, for the high meed of immortality.

Pretentiousness is risky; a vast, amorphous, self-generative anxiety comes with the equally vast and amorphous territory one has chosen to cover. One is highly susceptible to ridicule and possessed of such a number of flanks that it is impossible to protect them all. Since the size of one's ambitions is laid bare for the world to see, being thin-skinned is a predictable consequence and symptom of pretentiousness: One's skin is, after all, so painfully stretched over such a very large area. Implicit in grandiosity and pretentiousness is an unslakeable desire to embrace everyone. The impulse to make work that contains the world surely stems from an infantile impulse to swallow it, whole, and to be universally adored for having done so. These desires are even more doomed than the desires you develop as an adult, and to carry the appetite of an infant into middle age is to risk a certain indignity, to say the least (the way, for instance, that this speech attempts simultaneously a self-defense and a self-critique, and is I fear tangling itself up in knots). We pretentious writers of the Left share this unfortunate flaw, of being excessively thin-skinned and rapaciously greedy, with other control freaks, people we'd probably rather avoid any association with—Rush Limbaugh, Bob Dole, Adolf Hitler. . . .

Pretentiousness is, I sometimes think, a form of hysteria that manifests itself as listing, cataloging; manifests itself in a panicked strained effort towards the encyclopedic, lest the important ideas, which the pretentious writer doesn't feel she or he truly or deeply comprehends, escape while writerly attentions dazedly malinger over some bit of inconsequence.

But the joys of pretentiousness are more alluring than its humiliations are forbidding. It is as de Tocqueville says a profoundly democratic gesture, or failing, though not entirely as he understood it. Pretentiousness is in one sense a Promethean, protean liberation of the imagination, and anyone is capable of it, provided we pretenders can inure ourselves sufficiently to the shame that is heaped upon us when we are caught in the act of pretending. Pretentiousness consists in attempting an act of bold creation regardless of whether or not one has sufficient talent, emulating the daring of which only genius is truly capable—daring to see how close to the moon we are capable, all our insufficiencies and limitations notwithstanding, of soaring. Embracing pretentiousness as a trope, as a stratagem and a tool, becoming ironically aware rather than ashamed of grandiosity, enables us to make literary and perhaps political hay out of the distance between what we would like to have done, and what we have actually accomplished. The success and the failure both are part of the story, the success celebrating our gloriousness, the failure nobly demarcating our tragedy, but in both glory and tragedy, we pretenders are fabulous.

Pretentiousness is Camp, it is Drag, perhaps this is why it's most resplendently at home in the theater. Pretentiousness, *if it's done well*, performs a salutary parody of carving out, in the face of the theorilessness and bewilderment of our age, meta-narratives, legends, grand designs, even in spite of the suspiciousness with which we have learned, rightly, to regard meta-narrative: By pretending that such grandeur is still possible, we acknowledge how absolutely necessary, and indispensable, an overview, a theory, a big idea still is. Such Pretense will have to do, until the real thing comes along.

People fundamentally lacking a sense of humor when confronted with pretentiousness miss the irony and the fun and are left with flared nostrils indignantly aquiver at the *tastelessness* and the *presumption*. Invariably, such people are themselves guilty of pretention, and are drearily unaware of it.

To make political art is always to risk pretentiousness, because you can only ever fail to formulate answers to the questions you pose, if those questions are big enough—and really, if they aren't, why bother posing? To make overtly political art you must, I think, always declare more than you can prove and say more than you can know: You must speculate, and so risk the pretention all participatory political discourse is heir to. C. L. R. James values this most in Melville: the fact that Melville arrives at a place of self-confessed unknowing, that his art goes beyond his powers to explain, addressing issues of such depth that "to explain would be to dive deeper than Ishmael can go."

I suppose I am speaking here specifically of a tradition of public art that consciously engages itself with civic debate, a tradition of writing that, presumptuously, aspires to position itself among other grand American texts, each of which is not without its overreach. The Declaration of Independence is pretentious. So is the Constitution.

There is, of course, art that is not pretentious, just as there are of course good foods that are not overstuffed. There is, for instance, the matzoh: thin where the lasagna is fat, flat where the lasagna is thick, cold and dry and desert food where the lasagna is wet and steamy and Mediterranean, somber where the lasagna is meretricious; poverty versus richness. The matzoh is not pretentious; it is hard, brittle, transportable, it has been carried through the worst times imaginable, it is imaginably present, preparable, consumable in even the most dire of circumstances, and it evokes those circumstances even in the best of times. The matzoh is so formidable that no sooner does it make its appearance at the Passover Seder table than we slather it with a ragout of nuts, apples, honey, cinnamon and Shapiro's Kosher Wine (*"So thick you can cut it with a knife!"*)—because the matzoh reminds us: political success, stability, security, the luxury of time and ingredients needed to bake a lasagna, a play, a rounded identity: These things can and most likely will be stripped away, and you will be faced with hard choices. Cleave as bondsmen and women to the dangerous false beauty, the unrighteous magnificence of Mitzrayim; or go into the desert, liberated slaves, starved-tough and nourished on the harsh simple bread of haste and affliction.

The matzoh is a spiritual discipline, and it rebukes me each time I contemplate it that I am, or believe myself to be, incapable of such discipline; my instantaneous reflex when confronted with such ascetic, anhedonic bony reality is to grope blindly for the condiments, for the butter and salt, settling for whatever spice and lubrication comes first to hand. So as a playwright I find myself a determinedly optimistic baker of sloppy and runny and voluptuous concoctions, worried all the while that the exigencies of our times require a sparer, more sinewy approach. Leo Bersani and Ulysse Dutoit, in their wonderful book *Arts of Impoverishment*, describe the writing of Samuel Beckett, that matzoh of a playwright, this way: "In the ill-humored privacy of his art, in its defiant unrelatedness, Beckett reinvents our somewhat incomprehensible passage from the masochistic jouissance of self-enclosure to the fictional confusion of the 'I' and 'non-I.' At its very highest, art perhaps knows nothing but such confused beginnings, and in pushing us back to them it beneficently mocks the accumulated wisdom of culture."

For all that I have publicly decried the dangers of

assimilationism, for all that the assimilationism of the lesbian and gay Right infuriates me, I have long been guiltily aware of the extent to which my work and even my politics betray an assimilationist penchant for "the accumulated wisdom of culture," evident perhaps no place as clearly as in my ardent embrace of pretentiousness as my birthright as an American citizen, third generation ambivalently and only partially enfranchised— because queer—eternally implacably diasporan inhabitant in what my immigrant ancestors called Di Goldene Medina: land where even Jews get to bake lasagna—pork fennel sausage a weighty cultural and theological decision of course, and beef replaced by roasted eggplant if you're keeping milchedich and flechedich separate. Which, once they dismantle the FDA, kosher vegetarian might be the only way to go.

Recognizing the accumulated wisdom of culture as a repressive ideological apparatus is easy to do—read one of Bill Bennett's books, if you really hate yourself—but a radical rejection of aforesaid culture is more difficult. Imbedded in this culture is a history tending, though not deterministically, not without struggle, towards some plausible, workable, realizable version of radical, pluralist democracy. In American history and culture there is a liberal individualism which a radical anti-individualist progressivism relentlessly critiques and reshapes; a nonviolent, pragmatic revolutionary politics predicated on a collectivity of individuals reinventing themselves into something new; a social and economic justice emerging, fitfully; and for all our arrant and arid puritanism, a sensuality and a socialism of the skin. In American millenarianism I see the anticipation of the break that will finally

come when, even in this hard-hearted, bloody and mis-
trustful land, necessity finally submits, to borrow from
Akhmatova, and steps pensively aside.

I see the contradictory motions of this politics in
Melville, it's why he turns me on. Let me read you two
passages from his novel *White-Jacket*. These follow close
upon one another in the book: "Depravity in the
oppressed is no apology for the oppressor; but rather an
additional stigma to him, as being, in a larger degree, the
effect, and not the cause and justification of oppression."

This is formidable wisdom, arrived at in 1853; no one
in Washington today seems capable of it. But only a few
pages later Melville delivers himself of this vatic, imperial
pronouncement: "We Americans are the peculiar, chosen
people—the Israel of our time—God has given us, for a
future inheritance, the broad domains of the political
pagans. . . . The rest of the nations must soon be in our
rear. . . . With ourselves, almost for the first time in the
history of the earth, national selfishness is unbounded
philanthropy; for we cannot do a good to America but we
give alms to the world."

Here is something more congenial to the drafters
of the Contract With America. Melville at moments such
as these reminds us that pretentiousness, again, is an
expression of a certain luxuriousness, and hence
perhaps of privilege, and it is also an expression of aggressive power, of dominance—in this case, of a hegemonic
Manifest-Destiny-huffing-and-puffing that drowns out the
truths and the histories of noncitizens, of which the writer
is otherwise remarkably sensible. Both truth, and also the
lies State Power tells itself are present in Melville; like
Whitman, he contains multitudes. This naked, exposed

working-through, this public-arena-wrangling, is the cultural inheritance (more multiracial, multigendered, multi-preferenced an inheritance than the Right has ever understood) I cannot bring myself to abandon. Do I, in this reticence, betray myself as, God forbid, a liberal?

Many years ago in the famous AIDS issue of *October*, Leo Bersani, one of the authors of *Arts of Impoverishment*, published a provocatively titled, and provocative essay, "Is the Rectum a Grave?" Now Professor Bersani has published a new book called *Homos*. Let me read you a paragraph found on page 69:

> To move to an entirely different register, Tony Kushner's *Angels in America* has analogous ambitions. For Kushner, to be gay in the 1980s was to be a metaphor not only for Reagan's America but for the entire history of America, a country in which there are "no gods . . . no ghosts and spirits . . . no angels . . . no spiritual past, no racial past, there's only the political." The enormous success of this muddled and pretentious play is a sign, if we need still another one, of how ready and anxious America is to see and hear about gays—provided we reassure America how familiar, how morally sincere, and, particularly in the case of Kushner's work, how innocuously full of significance we can be.

Allow me to pause, before explaining why I am quoting this passage, to state that ten years have passed since that issue of *October* and I still don't know if the rectum is a grave, but I now think I have an answer to the question: Is Leo Bersani an asshole?

Yes, obviously, though not a stupid asshole. A college sophomore should know better than to try to build a case that being gay is, in my plays, a "metaphor" for anything, and hopefully that sophomore would be warned against the literary malpractice of quoting a character in a fiction as though he reliably speaks in the author's voice, especially while ignoring a context as laden with irony, and as significant to the reception of what the character is saying, as is the context in *Angels in America: Millennium Approaches* in which those quoted words are uttered. This nasty attack is uncharacteristic of the tenor of the rest of *Homos*—it's hurtful, of course, it's intended to be, but it's not the "muddled and pretentious" bit that bothers me especially. Muddled and pretentious are I think among the plays' *charms*, and as I said, people with no sense of humor don't like plays like mine; like de Tocqueville, Professor Bersani simply doesn't get it (he is, I might point out, a professor of French). I was more disturbed, and intrigued, by Professor Bersani's consternation over the fact that I offered the straight world representations of gay men who are "morally sincere." I plead guilty.

The reason I've decided to go through this, in addition to being, as I warned you, preternaturally, even *prenatally* thin-skinned, is that *Homos* offers itself as a critique of bourgeois lesbian and gay politics from a profoundly radical, subversive perspective. And as I have already pleaded guilty to assimilationist tendencies in my work, it would be disingenuous, now, to try to cast my plays as radical-as-they-ought-to-be. What's disturbing about *Homos*, and it seems to me disturbingly representative of at least a considerable portion of gay male radical thought, at least as it is expressed in literature, drama and queer theory, is that the antidote to the gay liberalism of which I am, perhaps, a deeply ambivalent example, is not, apparently, to be found in either socialism, or in more actively seeking and building common cause with other communities of the oppressed, or in the idea of community *period*.

In his penultimate chapter, "The Gay Outlaw," the professor begins with the question "Should the homosexual be a good citizen?" We already know, from the parts of the book we've already gotten through (and it is, I regret to say, a rather marvelous, exciting, infuriating and important book which raises a number of extremely important questions and formulates the problematics of identity politics elegantly) that Professor Bersani is going to answer this question, "Should the homosexual be a good citizen?" in the negative. He moves immediately from this question to the following statement: " . . . gay men and lesbians have been strenuously trying to persuade straight society that they can be good parents, good soldiers, good priests." Professor Bersani then confides that he "find[s] none of these options particularly stimulating . . ." The equation of good parenting with good soldiering is telling, as is the use of the word "stimulating." Moral sincerity is clearly not on his agenda. It is only a few pages later that we find Professor Bersani deep in an encomium to Jean Genêt, specifically stimulated by Genêt's "revolutionary strength": "Both [Genêt's] abhorrent glorification of Nazism [in *Funeral Rites*] and his in some ways equally abhorrent failure to take that glorification seriously express his fundamental project of declining to participate in any sociality at all. . . . *Funeral Rites* seeks to detach evil from its oppositional relation to good. . . . It would replace the rich social discursiveness of good-and-evil with what might be called the empty value of solitude."

In his preface, Professor Bersani has promised us a replacement for the "micropolitics of participatory democracy and social justice," which are to him "political ambitions as stirring as those reflected on the bumper stickers to 'think globally' and 'act locally.'" Instead of the *unstimulating* pursuit of democracy and social justice, Professor Bersani offers us this: "the most politically disruptive aspect of the homoness I will be exploring in gay desire is a redefinition of sociality so radical that it may appear to require a provisional withdrawal from relationality itself."

If you are confused, as I was, as to how a "provisional withdrawal from relationality," or as he later calls it, an "anti-communal mode of connectedness" can lead to effective oppositional politics, well, it doesn't. He continues, "This is not a political program. [The characters in *Funeral Rites*] are positioned for a reinventing of the social without any indication about how such a reinvention might proceed historically or what face it might have." This rejection is important, apparently, for "without such a rejection [of relationality], social revolt is doomed to repeat the oppressive conditions that provoked the revolt." Collective or communally based political engagement, in other words, is not simply insufficiently titillating, it is ultimately doomed, as Foucaultian complexities tuck opposition and resistance back within the inescapable context of those social practices against which resistance was conceived and initiated.

Homos, like the postmodernist texts it is heavily indebted to, is infinitely richer and more valuable than I perhaps understand and certainly more than I have time to explore. But there is something to be gleaned from the fact that the book begins as a critique of a political movement, begins by making queer theory's as-yet-to-be-redeemed promise of articulating notions of "the political productivity of the sexual," and concludes as a politically defeated, or at least politically *muddled*, celebration of books. If we were permitted to categorize Professor Bersani's politics as politics, we might venture ego-anarchism; as a psychological category (recognizing, of course, that such categories merely serve policing functions), sociopathy or autism comes to mind. Finally, though, this is a vision which, it seems to me, imprisons political struggle inside the pages of literature, from whence it does not emerge.

Beginning with a very important question for politically active homosexuals, namely "What is our *unique* contribution to progress to be?"; seeking to interrogate the life of desire as it flows through the Polity, and the subversive potential desire was once presumed to possess; recoiling from a politics of politeness that is willing to pathologize any and all desire that refuses to ape heterosexual norms, in exchange for lethal, powerless existence as recipients of *tolerance*—Professor Bersani arrives at a position in which, I would imagine, one would only avoid despair if one didn't care very much about the world to begin with.

Against the library-stillness of Professor Bersani's revolutionary defeatism ("This is Genêt's ingenious solution to the problem of revolutionary beginnings condemned to repeat old orders: he dies . . . "); against this ascertainably Left but not particularly invigorating implosional nonresponse to the present crisis, we can balance the spectacle, from the assimilationist camp, of one prominent gay citizen recently visiting a large Catholic midwestern campus, ostensibly for the purpose of critiquing the Church's homophobia, and in the process complimenting Joseph Cardinal Ratzinger for his "usual intellectual acerbity and indeed intellectual honesty," while the *New York Times* reporter covering the speech enthuses over the speaker's politeness, in the process equating ACT UP's anger with Operation Rescue's. Or another prominent gay citizen, one I admire a lot and who really should know better, offering the readers of the *New York Times*' Op-Ed page his opinion that ACT UP and GMHC share "some of the blame" for the fact that far too many of us have stopped practicing safe sex. ACT UP bashing, in fact, seems near-epidemic these days. Let's hope we aren't witnessing in such instances the beginnings of an old bad propensity for progressive people, when confronted with triumphant political evil, to take careful aim and shoot themselves in the feet.

We posit against these any politics, any theory that galvanizes action, that produces common cause, that is not self-defeating; perhaps, even, half-facetiously, half-seriously, a politics of literary pretentiousness, in which a book, or a play, muddled though it may be, is willing to sacrifice form and coherence in a determined effort to escape the library and become literature no longer—to become, instead, life. That this effort is also doomed, because writing will always remain writing, doesn't mean that the ultimate struggle is doomed or that writing has no contribution to make to a practical politics, to a ready response to the current unbelievable onslaught. The yearning displayed in pretentiousness may have its political uses, for one of the greatest dangers in times of reactionary backlash is that the borders of utopia appear to have been closed. When even bodily necessities are denied us we can too easily surrender the necessity of aspirations, dreams, hope—the future. Isn't any art that seeks to inspire or provoke or excite yearning likely to be, in some fashion, pretentious? And for a *sexual* politics, as our politics must necessarily be, is pretentiousness and its concomitant stirrings of no interest to the excesses of desire?

A politics that seeks to dismantle normalizing categories of gender; that seeks to retrieve a history from a violently enforced forgetting; a politics that seeks enfranchisement not only for new kinds of citizens, but for Sexuality itself, that seeks to introduce fucking and sucking, licking and smelling, kink, sleaze, clits and dicks and tits and assholes and the games people play with them, into the previously chaste Temple of Democracy; and even more daring still, a politics that seeks a synthesis between desire and transformation, that seeks some union between the deepest recesses and cavities of the human heart and body and soul, and the sacrifices and responsibilities building communities and movement, building progress and power entails: This politics needs its writers, and its writers had better be capable of extravagance, had better not be tame.

Oh well who knows, really? Talk about pretentiousness!

I have to end, I have to end, last year you couldn't get me here and now you can't get me to shut up. The offer for lasagna still stands. Last year, a few weeks after OutWrite, I was stopped on lower Broadway by two adorable men who demanded that I take them home and feed them lasagna. I, sexually flusterable as always in the face of a challenge or opportunity, let them slip away, but the encounter has left pasta charged with scintillations of the erotic. You should all come over, I will cook for you all. Except now I'm vegetarian. *Oh I am so glad this is over!* If I've made a fool of myself, I have at least made of myself the kind of fool I want to be: That is the virtue and power of pretentiousness.

I'll wrap up with Blake, that most unpityingly pretentious or rather *grandiose* of poets—because it can't really be called pretentious if it was dictated to you by angels: "I pretend not to Holiness; yet I pretend to love. . . . Therefore dear reader, *forgive* what you do not approve, & *love* me for the energetic exertion of my talent."

I promise you I will love you all for the energetic exertion of yours.

See you in Washington. See you on the Internet. See you on the streets.

Thank you.

SLAVS!

▼

*Thinking About the
Longstanding Problems of
Virtue and Happiness*

A SHORT PLAY IN A PROLOGUE,
THREE ACTS AND
AN EPILOGUE

This play is for Oskar Eustis,
beloved comrade.

ACKNOWLEDGMENTS

I'm very grateful to Jon Jory and Michael Bigelow Dixon for commissioning this play and making it possible for me to complete it.

In its final shape and for many individual moments of staging, *Slavs!*, and its author, owe a lot to Lisa Peterson, who directed it hot off the laser printer at the Actors Theatre of Louisville, and in its New York incarnation.

Slavs! (Thinking About the Longstanding Problems of Virtue and Happiness) was commissioned and first presented by the Actors Theatre of Louisville as part of the 1994 Humana Festival of New American Plays in Louisville, Kentucky. The production, under the direction of Lisa Peterson, opened March 8, 1994, with the following cast:

VASSILY VOROVILICH SMUKOV	Michael Kevin
SERGE ESMERELDOVICH UPGOBKIN	Gerald Hiken
ALEKSII ANTEDILLUVIANOVICH PRELAPSARIANOV	Ray Fry
IPPOLITE IPPOPOLITOVICH POPOLITIPOV	Fred Major
YEGOR TREMENS RODENT	Steven Culp
KATHERINA SERAFIMA GLEB	Kate Goehring
BONFILA BEZHUKHOVNA BONCH-BRUEVICH	Mary Shultz
MRS. SHASTLIVYI DOMIK	Barbara eda-Young
VODYA DOMIK	Annie-Laurie Audenaert

On June 6, 1994, a staged reading of *Slavs!* was given as a benefit for the Lesbian Avengers Civil Rights Organizing Project at the Walter Kerr Theatre in New York City. The reading was produced by David Binder, James Calleri and David G. O'Connell. Michael Mayer directed the following cast:

FIRST BABUSHKA	Ellen McLaughlin
SECOND BABUSHKA	Sherry Glaser
VASSILY VOROVILICH SMUKOV	Anne Pitoniak
SERGE ESMERELDOVICH UPGOBKIN	Olympia Dukakis
ALEKSII ANTEDILLUVIANOVICH	
PRELAPSARIANOV	Kathleen Chalfant
IPPOLITE IPPOPOLITOVICH POPOLITIPOV	Tracey Ullman
YEGOR TREMENS RODENT	Madeline Kahn
KATHERINA SERAFIMA GLEB	Sandra Bernhard
BONFILA BEZHUKHOVNA	
BONCH-BRUEVICH	Laurie Metcalf
MRS. SHASTLIVYI DOMIK	Barbara eda-Young
VODYA DOMIK	Annie-Laurie Audenaert
NARRATOR	Kate Clinton
HOST	Tabitha Soren
SPEAKER	Sheila Quinn

(This reading was recorded and will be available on CD from Simon & Schuster.)

In June 1994, *Slavs!* was produced by the Steppenwolf Theatre Company in Chicago. Eric Simonson directed the following cast:

VASSILY VOROVILICH SMUKOV	Bernie Landis
SERGE ESMERELDOVICH UPGOBKIN	Jim Mohr
ALEKSII ANTEDILLUVIANOVICH	
PRELAPSARIANOV	Nathan Davis
IPPOLITE IPPOPOLITOVICH POPOLITIPOV	Bradley Mott

YEGOR TREMENS RODENT	William J. Norris
KATHERINA SERAFIMA GLEB	Mariann Mayberry
BONFILA BEZHUKHOVNA BONCH-BRUEVICH	Amy Morton
MRS. SHASTLIVYI DOMIK	Martha Lavey
VODYA DOMIK	Heather Marie Johnson

The play opened in New York City at New York Theatre Workshop in November 1994. Lisa Peterson directed the following cast:

VASSILY VOROVILICH SMUKOV	Ben Hammer
SERGE ESMERELDOVICH UPGOBKIN	Gerald Hiken
ALEKSII ANTEDILLUVIANOVICH PRELAPSARIANOV	Joseph Wiseman
IPPOLITE IPPOPOLITOVICH POPOLITIPOV	John Christopher Jones
YEGOR TREMENS RODENT	David Chandler
KATHERINA SERAFIMA GLEB	Marisa Tomei
BONFILA BEZHUKHOVNA BONCH-BRUEVICH	Mary Shultz
MRS. SHASTLIVYI DOMIK	Barbara eda-Young
VODYA DOMIK	Mischa Barton

In December 1994, *Slavs!* opened in London at the Hampstead Theatre. Matthew Lloyd directed the following cast:

| VASSILY VOROVILICH SMUKOV | Peter Bayliss |
| SERGE ESMERELDOVICH UPGOBKIN | Richard Mayes |

ALEKSII ANTEDILLUVIANOVICH	
PRELAPSARIANOV	Peter Copley
IPPOLITE IPPOPOLITOVICH POPOLITIPOV	Paul Jesson
YEGOR TREMENS RODENT	Ron Cook
KATHERINA SERAFIMA GLEB	Aisling O'Sullivan
BONFILA BEZHUKHOVNA	
BONCH-BRUEVICH	Imelda Staunton
MRS. SHASTLIVYI DOMIK	Annette Badland
VODYA DOMIK	Carly Maker and Lucy Kent

Slavs! was co-produced by Center Stage in Baltimore, Maryland (January 6–February 18, 1995) and Yale Repertory Theatre in New Haven, Connecticut (February 24–March 18, 1995). Lisa Peterson directed the following cast:

VASSILY VOROVILICH SMUKOV	James J. Lawless
SERGE ESMERELDOVICH UPGOBKIN	James Greene
ALEKSII ANTEDILLUVIANOVICH	
PRELAPSARIANOV	Ronny Graham
IPPOLITE IPPOPOLITOVICH POPOLITIPOV	Lee Wilkof
YEGOR TREMENS RODENT	Christopher McCann
KATHERINA SERAFIMA GLEB	Katie MacNichol
BONFILA BEZHUKHOVNA	
BONCH-BRUEVICH	Caitlin O'Connell
MRS. SHASTLIVYI DOMIK	Ludmila Bokievsky
VODYA DOMIK	Meredith Friend (CS)
	Maren E. Rosenberg (CS)
	Sarah Moore Brochin (YRT)

CHARACTERS

FIRST BABUSHKA: a snow sweep of indeterminate age.

SECOND BABUSHKA: another snow sweep of indeterminate age.

VASSILY VOROVILICH SMUKOV: a high-ranking Politburo member, a pessimistic man in his seventies.

SERGE ESMERELDOVICH UPGOBKIN: a high-ranking Politburo member, an optimistic man in his eighties.

ALEKSII ANTEDILLUVIANOVICH PRELAPSARIANOV: a Politburo member of incalculable rank, the world's oldest living Bolshevik, considerably older than ninety.

IPPOLITE IPPOPOLITOVICH POPOLITIPOV: an apparatchik of some importance, a sour man in his sixties.

YEGOR TREMENS RODENT: an apparatchik of less importance, attached to Popolitipov; a nervous type in his fifties.

KATHERINA SERAFIMA GLEB: a security guard at the Pan-Soviet Archives for the Study of Cerebro-Cephalognomical Historico-Biological Materialism (also known as PASOVACERCEPHHIBIMAT). An inebriated young woman in her twenties.

BONFILA BEZHUKHOVNA BONCH-BRUEVICH: a pediatric oncologist, a pleasant woman in her thirties.

BIG BABUSHKA: yet another snow sweep of indeterminate age, garrulous, large, with a moustache.

MRS. SHASTLIVYI DOMIK: an unhappy, angry woman in her forties.

VODYA DOMIK: a silent little girl, eight years old.

The play takes place in Moscow, March 1985; and Talmenka, Siberia, 1992.

Author's Notes

For the information on the Soviet nuclear catastrophe which is addressed in Act Three, I am indebted primarily to a series of articles by John-Thor Dahlburg which ran in the *Los Angeles Times*, September 2–4, 1992; to Grigori Medvedev's *The Truth About Chernobyl*; and to Dr. Don Pizzarello of New York University Medical Center.

IN PERFORMANCE: The actors should probably use very, very mild Russian accents—standard American accents, really, lightly perfumed with something Slavic. But intelligibility is paramount—so don't eliminate diphthongs or replace too many *w*'s with *v*'s.

ALSO IN PERFORMANCE: The First and Second Babushkas should be played by the actresses playing Dr. Bonch-Bruevich and Mrs. Domik. The Big Babushka should be played by the actor playing Smukov.

AND ANOTHER THING: Status is very important. Prelapsarianov is the highest-ranking Politburo member of the five; Upgobkin is next; then Smukov (probably a military man); then, lower by several degrees, Popolitipov; then, lowest of all, Rodent. The lesser are careful with, and polite to, the greater. Popolitipov is incomparably more powerful than Katherina, who pays no attention to the fact. He is more powerful than, and also dangerous to, Bonfila, who is acutely aware of this. In Act Three, Rodent is now the goodwill ambassador of a democratically elected federal government, the problem being that Rodent has no good will, and he both bitterly resents and desperately needs his job; and, in addition to the coward he has always been, he has become a closet fascist. For Bonch-Bruevich and Mrs. Domik, he is the first representative of real power they've seen, in years, and as such is both an opportunity and a target for their great frustration, rage and grief.

The stakes are very high.

THE FIRST ACT IS TREACHEROUS!

The first act is delicate. It's a big mistake to strain towards big laughs in the first few scenes. This is not a farce, not a knockabout comedy! When the play is being performed you have to remember that the audience is being ushered instantly into an unfamiliar world—the accents, the history, the theoretical, rhetorical, poetic speech, the political, moral, romantic passion are all unfamiliar; and the audience must be relaxed in order to listen to what the characters are saying. And the most important thing is that the ideas are clear, that the language sings. The action of much of the first act is *to think*—about the longstanding problems of virtue and happiness—a lively, active, vigorous, passionate thinking, not introspective brooding, but *thinking hard, discussing*.

I suggest a flexibly hieratic staging of the scene in Act One, according to which the actors are grouped in arrangements that help make the argument clear, that reveal the position each character represents on the political spectrum—for instance, that the real dialectic here is between Upgobkin (true progress) and Popolitipov (true reaction), with Smukov and Rodent trying to keep up, and Prelapsarianov representing a third term, a synthesis. These are all people who speak their thoughts, rather than people who think and then speak. There is no need for pausing to arrive at an idea or an articulation—rhetorical grandeur is second nature for them, expressive of great Slavic passion. However, the lack of struggle to find words does not mean that the specific words they choose are unimportant to them—language is everything. As is politics, the air they breathe; as is love.

CASTING: The play's been done in a number of ways: one actor, age and gender appropriate, per part; but also with a wonderful all-female cast, and now Michael Greif is doing it at La Jolla Playhouse with five adult actors (Poppy and Rodent are men, the other parts are played by three women) and the child. I think that a certain inventiveness in casting can be a good thing for the play.

If it seems desirable to help the audience know where it is (I recommend it), taped voice-over introductions can be played before the following scenes:

Before Act One, Scene 1

VOICE ON TAPE

(Russian accent, of course) An anteroom outside the Chamber of Deputies, the Kremlin. Moscow, March 1985.

Before Act One, Scene 2

(On tape the babble of hundreds of voices arguing passionately. The sound of a gavel pounding the rostrum in an immense hall. The crowd gets quieter but not silent. A voice exclaims:)

VOICE ON TAPE

Comrades! Comrades! Aleksii Antedilluvianovich Prelapsarianov! *(Then in a whisper)* The world's oldest living Bolshevik . . .

Before Act Two, Scene 1

VOICE ON TAPE

The guards' chamber of the Pan-Soviet Archives for the Study of Cerebro-Cephalognomical Historico-Biological Materialism, also known as PASOVACERCEPHHIBIMAT. Moscow, March 1985.

(Note: PASOVACERCEPHHIBIMAT is pronounced "passovah-sayr-seff-HIB-i-mat.")

Before Act Three, Scene 1

VOICE ON TAPE

A medical facility. Talmenka, Siberia, 1992.

PROLOGUE

▼

The idea of socialism, as the word itself indicates, is based on the idea and the practice of *a society*. This may seem, at first sight, to do nothing to distinguish it from other political ideas, but that is only because we haven't looked closely enough. The very idea of *a society*—that is, a definite form of human relationships in certain specific conditions at a particular moment in history—is itself comparatively modern. *Society* used to mean mainly the company of other people. The idea of *a society* was to distinguish one form of social relationships from another, and to show that these forms varied historically and could change. Thus, in thinking about the longstanding problems of virtue and happiness, people who began from the idea of a society did not immediately refer the problems to a general human nature or to inevitable conditions of existence; they looked first at the precise forms of the society in which they were living and at how these might, where necessary, be changed.

—RAYMOND WILLIAMS
"Walking Backwards into the Future"

(Two babushkas, dressed in knee-length cheap winter coats, their legs encased in thick white support hose, their feet shod in rubber galoshes, their heads of course wrapped in floral- or geometric-print scarves tied under the chin, are sweeping snow from the entrance steps of the Hall of the Soviets, the Kremlin, March 1985. As they sweep, the snow falls; they talk.)

FIRST BABUSHKA

However reluctant one may be to grant it, history and the experience of this century presses upon us the inescapable conclusion that there is a direct continuum from Dictatorship of the Proletariat and the embrace of violence as a means of effecting change that one finds in later Marx and Engels to dictatorship plain and simple—you missed a spot—and state terror.

SECOND BABUSHKA

True enough. But Marx's defense of revolutionary violence must be set in its proper context, namely: the nineteenth-century evolutionary-socialist error-of-belief in the Inevitability of Gradualism, which sought not so much to transform society into something new . . .

FIRST BABUSHKA

. . . But rather to create merely an "improved" version of the society one sought to change.

SECOND BABUSHKA

Exactly.

FIRST BABUSHKA

But is it not a false antinomy to predicate as the only alternative to Reformism or Gradualism a vanguard-driven . . .

(*Two Politburo members, V. V. Smukov and S. E. Upgobkin, very impressive in greatcoats and big fur hats, enter.*)

SECOND BABUSHKA

(*Seeing them*) Shhhh! Shhhhhh!

(*The babushkas clam up tight. They sweep.*)

VASSILY VOROVILICH SMUKOV

Morning grandma.

(*The babushkas suddenly become sweet, toothless old ladies, smiling, head-bobbing, forelock-tugging mumblers.*)

FIRST BABUSHKA

Good morning sirs!

SECOND BABUSHKA

How-de-doo! Mind the ice, don't slip!

(*Upgobkin and Smukov start up the steps.*)

FIRST BABUSHKA

Big doings today, sirs . . .

VASSILY VOROVILICH SMUKOV

Oh, the usual Mischief . . .

SERGE ESMERELDOVICH UPGOBKIN

(*Watching them sweep*) Heavy snows for March. Your labor, I fear, is *Sisyphean!*

SECOND BABUSHKA

And what's more, sir, it's *completely pointless!* We sweep, it falls, we sweep some more, it falls some more . . .

FIRST BABUSHKA

It's hopeless, hopeless!

(*The two babushkas laugh and laugh.*)

VASSILY VOROVILICH SMUKOV

That's the spirit, grandma! Sweep! Sweep!

(*The babushkas sweep; they are all laughing. Smukov and Upgobkin take each other's arm, climb the stairs and disappear into the Hall. The babushkas instantly stop laughing.*)

FIRST BABUSHKA

So where was I?

SECOND BABUSHKA

. . . a vanguard-driven . . .

FIRST BABUSHKA

Yes! A vanguard-driven revolution as the only alternative to Reaction. For the People make their own history.

SECOND BABUSHKA

Limits are set by the conditions of their social development.

FIRST BABUSHKA

But those conditions are themselves affected by the state
of their economic relations. (*She stops sweeping.*)
Sweeping snow. In Moscow. It *is* sisyphean.

SECOND BABUSHKA

(*A shrug*) Nevertheless. *Sweep*, "grandma."

FIRST BABUSHKA

Grandma yourself. (*Sweeping again.*)
Big doings today . . .

SECOND BABUSHKA

Big.

ACT ONE

▼

"O tell me of the Russians, Communist, my son!
Tell me of the Russians, my honest young man!"
"They are moving for the people, mother; let me alone,
For I'm worn out with reading
and want to lie down."

—JOHN BERRYMAN
"Communist"

SCENE 1

(*In an anteroom outside the Politburo Chamber in the Hall of the Soviets in the Kremlin. March 1985. Smukov and Upgobkin, in suits now, are sitting and talking. A samovar stands nearby, brewing tea.*)

VASSILY VOROVILICH SMUKOV

People are not capable of change.

They used to be, maybe, but not anymore. In the old days you could ask anything of the people and they'd do it: Live without bread, without heat in the winter, take a torch to their own houses—as long as they believed they were building socialism there was no limit to how much they could adapt, transform. Moldable clay in the hands of history.

SERGE ESMERELDOVICH UPGOBKIN

And you feel it's different now?

VASSILY VOROVILICH SMUKOV

Well, you see.

We are all grown less pliable, unsure of our footing, unsure of the way, brittle bones and cataracts . . .
How are your cataracts, by the way, Serge Esmereldovich?

SERGE ESMERELDOVICH UPGOBKIN

(*Shrugs*) Old eyes get tough, cloudy. This one (*Points to one eye*) is not really an eye anymore, it's a bottle cork, it's a walnut. This one (*Points to the other eye*) lets in milky light. I live in a world of milk-white ghosts now, luminous beings, washed clean of detail. And I hear better, Vashka: in every voice, a million voices whispering. (*Imitates whispering; it sounds like the sea*) Sssssshhhhh, shhssshhh . . . More tea?

VASSILY VOROVILICH SMUKOV

No; I'll have to get up to pee in the middle of Aleksii's speech.

SERGE ESMERELDOVICH UPGOBKIN

Whereas I intend to drink two more cups, so the pressure on my bladder will keep me awake.

VASSILY VOROVILICH SMUKOV

At least in the bad old days you could sleep through the speeches and not worry that you'd miss a thing. Now the speeches are longer and you have to stay awake to boo. It's miserable: democracy. Grishin or Gorbachev, Gorbachev or Grishin. I vote *not* to vote! I am a true apostle of the old scientific creed: Geriatrical Materialism. Our motto: Stagnation is our only hope. Our sacred text: silence. Not this interminable debate, blah blah blah, my side, your side—really, this is logorrhea, not revolution.

SERGE ESMERELDOVICH UPGOBKIN

Patience.

There are no shortcuts to the new era. The terrain is vast. Aeons to traverse, everything is implicated, everything encompassed, the world, the universe . . .

Today this anteroom is the anteroom to History, Vashka! Beyond those doors, inside that chamber, History is aborning! Inhale its perfumes! A harsh and unnaturally protracted winter is losing its teeth. A great pressure has built up to this, Vashka, a great public desperation. There is no choice. You'll see that people can change, and change radically. From crown to toe, every cell formed anew. We set the process in motion with our words.

VASSILY VOROVILICH SMUKOV

People, I think, would rather die than change.

SERGE ESMERELDOVICH UPGOBKIN

Do you really think so?

I believe precisely the opposite.

We would rather change than die.

We have been ordered into motion by History herself, Vashka. When the sun comes out, the sky cracks open, the silent flowers twist and sway . . .

SCENE 2

(Aleksii Antedilluvianovich Prelapsarianov, the world's oldest Bolshevik, speaking in the Chamber of Deputies. He is unimaginably old and totally blind; his voice is thin and high, but he speaks with great passion.)

ALEKSII ANTEDILLUVIANOVICH PRELAPSARIANOV

And *Theory? Theory?* How are we to proceed without *Theory?* Is it enough to reject the past, is it wise to move forward in this blind fashion, without the Cold Brilliant Light of Theory to guide the way? What have these reformers to offer in the way of Theory? What beautiful system of thought have they to present to the world, to the befuddling, contrary tumult of life, to this mad swirling planetary disorganization, to the Inevident Welter of fact, event, phenomenon, calamity? Do they have, as we did, a beautiful Theory, as bold, as Grand, as comprehensive a construct . . . ? You can't imagine, when we first read the Classic Texts, when in the dark vexed night of our ignorance and terror the seed-words sprouted and shoved incomprehension aside, when the incredible bloody vegetable struggle up and through into Red Blooming gave us Praxis, True Praxis, True Theory married to Actual Life . . . You who live in this Sour Little Age cannot imagine the sheer grandeur of the prospect we gazed upon: like standing atop the highest peak in the mighty Caucasus, and viewing in one all-knowing glance the mountainous, granite order of creation. We were One with the Sidereal Pulse then, in the blood in our heads we heard the tick of the Infinite. You cannot imagine it. I weep for you.

And what have you to offer now, children of this Theory? What have you to offer in its place? Market Incentives? Watered-down Bukharinite stopgap makeshift Capitalism? NEPmen! Pygmy children of a gigantic race!

Change? Yes, we must must change, only show me the Theory, and I will be at the barricades, show me the book of the next Beautiful Theory, and I promise you these blind eyes will see again, just to read it, to devour that text. Show me the words that will reorder the world, or else keep silent.

The snake sheds its skin only when a new skin is ready; if he gives up the only membrane he has before he can replace it, naked he will be in the world, prey to the forces of chaos: without his skin he will be dismantled, lose coherence and die. Have you, my little serpents, a new skin?

Then we dare not, we cannot move ahead.

Scene 3

(*Outside the Chamber of Deputies again, the Kremlin. Ippolite Ippopolitovich Popolitipov and Yegor Tremens Rodent, two middle-aged deputies, are talking. Popolitipov is in a rage over the debate in the adjoining chamber. Rodent is freaked out. Rodent is Popolitipov's protégé, and is profoundly deferential.*)

IPPOLITE IPPOPOLITOVICH POPOLITIPOV
The heart is not progressive. The heart is conservative, no matter what the mind may be. Why don't they get that? The mind may make its leaps ahead; the heart will refuse to budge, shatter at the prospect. Yearn to go back to what it loves. That's the function of the organ, that's what it's there for: to fall in love. And love is profoundly reactionary, you fall in love and that instant is fixed, love is always fixed on the past.

YEGOR TREMENS RODENT

Oh true. Oh I am all terror these days. Sleep with the light on. No idea of what: just terror. Popolitipov, look! I'm shaking!

IPPOLITE IPPOPOLITOVICH POPOLITIPOV

Now debate that, reformers! The conservative, fractable human heart!

(Serge Esmereldovich Upgobkin enters, leading Aleksii Antedilluvianovich Prelapsarianov to a comfy chair.)

YEGOR TREMENS RODENT

(To Popolitipov) Sssshhhh.

(Popolitipov and Rodent move a discreet distance away from the two old Bolsheviks.)

ALEKSII ANTEDILLUVIANOVICH PRELAPSAPIANOV

(As Upgobkin helps him to his chair) Stop hovering, Serge Esmereldovich, you're practically buggering me!

SERGE ESMERELDOVICH UPGOBKIN

I have to stand this close, otherwise I don't see . . .

ALEKSII ANTEDILLUVIANOVICH PRELAPSAPIANOV

Nothing to see! I'm fine! And your breath is terrible. Please, you give me the fidgets. It's just a vein, just a weak vein in my head.

SERGE ESMERELDOVICH UPGOBKIN

I'll get some tea for you . . . *(Looking about)* If I can find the samovar.

YEGOR TREMENS RODENT

There, comrade Upgobkin, it's over there . . .

ALEKSII ANTEDILLUVIANOVICH PRELAPSAPIANOV

I'm the blind one! You just have cataracts! I'm *blind*!

IPPOLITE IPPOPOLITOVICH POPOLITIPOV

Is Comrade Minister Prelapsarianov not feeling well?

ALEKSII ANTEDILLUVIANOVICH PRELAPSAPIANOV

HOURS! HOURS OF TALK! What do they think they have to say! Such pretentiousness, they fart and they whinny and I HAVE AN ANEURISM! (*He has gotten overexcited*) Oh, oh, oh . . .

SERGE ESMERELDOVICH UPGOBKIN

Some hot tea . . . (*He pours in a stiff shot of vodka from a hip flask.*)

IPPOLITE IPPOPOLITOVICH POPOLITIPOV

(*Quietly, to Rodent*) For decades a mostly respectable torpor. Now: Expect madness.

YEGOR TREMENS RODENT

(*Also quiet*) In Omsk thousands saw a radiant orb in the sky, larger than the moon. Sea monsters were seen swimming in some Kazakhstan lake. Strange space creatures reported landed in Gorki . . .

IPPOLITE IPPOPOLITOVICH POPOLITIPOV

With three eyes. And they marched about the square.

YEGOR TREMENS RODENT

Six eyes. Tiny tiny head, big big body, six eyes.

IPPOLITE IPPOPOLITOVICH POPOLITIPOV

I really think it was only three.

YEGOR TREMENS RODENT

Two rows of three each, which makes six.

IPPOLITE IPPOPOLITOVICH POPOLITIPOV

Aha.

SERGE ESMERELDOVICH UPGOBKIN

(*Offering the teacup to Prelapsarianov*) Can you swallow it?

ALEKSII ANTEDILLUVIANOVICH PRELAPSAPIANOV

My head, my head, inside my brain, there's an itch, a little worm . . . Sssshhhh. Sssshhhh . . . (*He cradles his head.*)

YEGOR TREMENS RODENT

The theory is that radioactivity escaped from the explosion at the plutonium plant at Mayak is calling to them, the creatures, from across space, and they come perhaps with food and magic farm equipment, or personal computers, or with death rays to kill us all, and in Novy Sibirsk, people whose grandparents were merely babies when the Czar was killed are rumored to have used black arts to resurrect . . . Rasputin. *Rasputin.*

IPPOLITE IPPOPOLITOVICH POPOLITIPOV

This cannot be what Lenin intended.

YEGOR TREMENS RODENT

Fantasy is the spiritual genius of Slavic peoples.
And icons weep blood again. As if seventy years of socialism had never happened at all.

ALEKSII ANTEDILLUVIANOVICH PRELAPSAPIANOV

(*Sitting suddenly bolt upright*) Wait. Wait. OH! OH!

SERGE ESMERELDOVICH UPGOBKIN

Aleksii? Aleksii!

YEGOR TREMENS RODENT

Is Comrade Minister all right, is . . .

(*Aleksii Antedilluvianovich stands, staring ahead, dropping the teacup.*)

IPPOLITE IPPOPOLITOVICH POPOLITIPOV

Serge Esmereldovich, is he . . . ?

ALEKSII ANTEDILLUVIANOVICH PRELAPSAPIANOV

I see it now! Now I see! For ninety years I have wondered and wondered and wondered WHY is the Good Cause always defeated by the Bad, WHY Injustice and never Justice anywhere, WHY does Evil always always triumph and Good cast down in the gutter to be shat upon, WHY THIS HORROR AND WHY THIS HEARTACHE and NOW I GET IT! Because God . . . is a Menshevik! Because God . . . is a Petty-Bourgeois! Because God is a Reactionary, and Progressive People are THE POLITICAL ENEMIES OF GOD! He HATES US! Now! Now AT LAST I SEE— (*He collapses and dies.*)

SERGE ESMERELDOVICH UPGOBKIN

Aleksii? Aleksii!?

YEGOR TREMENS RODENT

Oh my God . . .

SERGE ESMERELDOVICH UPGOBKIN

Oh help, oh help, oh somebody, somebody, Aleksii Antedilluvianovich Prelapsarianov is dead!

SCENE 4

(Smukov enters.)

VASSILY VOROVILICH SMUKOV

Did I hear . . . ?
Oh my. A dead body.

SERGE ESMERELDOVICH UPGOBKIN

Aleksii Antedilluvianovich Prelapsarianov is dead.

VASSILY VOROVILICH SMUKOV

Oh dear, he spoke too long. So many words, we were afraid this might happen.

IPPOLITE IPPOPOLITOVICH POPOLITIPOV

The strain on the heart.

YEGOR TREMENS RODENT

No, it was his brain. A vessel popped upstairs. His face is royal purple.

IPPOLITE IPPOPOLITOVICH POPOLITIPOV

But popped because: The grieving heart avenged itself on the forward-moving mind. The heart drowned the brain in blood. So that the whole animal could rest, safe from the future, secure in the past. As I was saying, the mind may . . .

YEGOR TREMENS RODENT

Someone ought to call security, we can't leave him lying . . .

SERGE ESMERELDOVICH UPGOBKIN

His heart had little reason to murder his mind, Ippolite Ippopolitovich, Aleksii's mind was hardly moving in a forward direction.

VASSILY VOROVILICH SMUKOV

I thought in the main his arguments were sound. As I understood it . . .

IPPOLITE IPPOPOLITOVICH POPOLITIPOV

The brain inhabits the body like a virus inhabits a cell. It takes control of the nucleus and selfishly mismanages the entirety till disaster results. It does not do to think too much! You reformers, you vanguard, you taskmaster brain . . .

YEGOR TREMENS RODENT

Oh you are making too much of this, Poppy, Comrade Minister Prelapsarianov was ninety-five years old. No wonder, it was past his time.

IPPOLITE IPPOPOLITOVICH POPOLITIPOV

Illness is a metaphor, Yegor; the human body, the body politic, the human soul, the soul of the state. Dynamic and immobile all at once, lava and granite, the head and the heart. It's all tension and tearing, and which will win? An infarction *(Clutches his heart)* or a stroke? *(Clutches his head.)*

VASSILY VOROVILICH SMUKOV

I don't know what you're talking about, Popolitipov, but one thing is clear: We should not move until we know where we're going. They should chisel that on poor Aleksii's tombstone, that was his best bit. Wait patiently till the way is clear.

SERGE ESMERELDOVICH UPGOBKIN

And imagination? That faculty? Which Angels are said to lack, but people possess? Dialectics can only lead us so far, to the edge of what is known. But after that . . . ? We see so poorly, almost blind. We who . . .

YEGOR TREMENS RODENT

Careful, Serge Esmereldovich, if you're going to make a speech, look at what happened to poor Comrade Minister, and you're almost as old as he is . . . was.

SERGE ESMERELDOVICH UPGOBKIN

Then let me follow him into oblivion. Let me make that leap. Because you can only creep so far, and then you must leap, Rodent, you must use your own legs and your own will, or life itself will simply toss you in the air, but willing or resisting, I promise you all, you will leap! Does the heart plot to kill the mind, does it shatter that not-sprouted seed, the brain, before the New Blooms blossom? Then let the heart beware, for my brain will dream the New, I will make that leap, and let the strain be too much, let the strain explode my recalcitrant heart, let my heart burst like a bomb while my sparks leap their synapses! We must dream the New! And by Caution we never can! By Leaping! (*He begins to leap in the air, over and over, going higher and higher.*)

IPPOLITE IPPOPOLITOVICH POPOLITIPOV
Stop it, Serge Esmereldovich Upgobkin, you'll . . .

SERGE ESMERELDOVICH UPGOBKIN
(*As he leaps, to Popolitipov*) Leap, you unregenerate Stalinist! Leap, you bursitic Brezhnevite! Leap, leap, Procrustean, legless Legachevite, leap!
So what if they dissolve the entire Union, so what if the Balkans are all re-Balkanized, so what if the Ukraine won't sell us their wheat, and Georgia secedes, and Germany reunites, and all our reforms go only to squelch real revolution!

VASSILY VOROVILICH SMUKOV
Oh, well, now that would really be terrible, we . . .

SERGE ESMERELDOVICH UPGOBKIN
(*Still leaping, continuing over the above, to Smukov*) LEAP! HIGH! See if you can see it! The NEW! The UNIMAG-INED! The THAT-FOR-WHICH-OUR-DREAMS-ARE-ACHING! For what is hope but desiring forwards!? (*To Rodent*) Are you a man, or are you a mollusc? Will you never dare? Will you be dead forever?

YEGOR TREMENS RODENT
NO!

SERGE ESMERELDOVICH UPGOBKIN

Then LEAP!

(Upgobkin and Rodent leap and leap.)

VASSILY VOROVILICH SMUKOV

Serge, Serge, please don't overexert yourself, what has gotten into you?

SERGE ESMERELDOVICH UPGOBKIN

The NEW! The NEW! The NEW!

IPPOLITE IPPOPOLITOVICH POPOLITIPOV

(Over the above) Yegor Tremens Rodent, stop that at once!

(Popolitipov stops Rodent, pulls him down to earth.)

IPPOLITE IPPOPOLITOVICH POPOLITIPOV

Control yourself, dammit.

VASSILY VOROVILICH SMUKOV

Look at him! Serge . . .

(Upgobkin is leaping higher and higher. His face is upturned, he is no longer with his comrades, he is beatific, he is smiling enormously.
From above there is a violently brief burst of radiance, and the instant it falls on Upgobkin he collapses and dies. And the light is gone.)

YEGOR TREMENS RODENT

Now I am calling security. And no more metaphors, any-one, please.
Two bodies, two bodies, what a scandal this will make.

IPPOLITE IPPOPOLITOVICH POPOLITIPOV

Was it his heart, or was it his head?

YEGOR TREMENS RODENT

Heart.

VASSILY VOROVILICH SMUKOV

Still smiling. That smile. What on earth do you suppose he saw?

(They look up, wondering.)

ACT TWO

▼

"That's why I loved you, for your magnanimous
heart! And you do not need my forgiveness, nor
I yours; it's all the same whether you forgive or not,
all my life you will remain a wound in my soul,
and I in yours—that's how it should be."

—FYODOR DOSTOEVSKY
The Brothers Karamazov
(*Translated by Richard Pevear and
Larissa Volokhonsky*)

And, oh, how blue the cornflowers,
how black the earth, how red the kerchief
of the female comrade!

—JOHN ASH
"A History of Soviet Organ Music"

Scene 1

(*In the small, dank, dark, dismal room that serves as the guards' chamber of the Pan-Soviet Archives for the Study of Cerebro-Cephalognomical Historico-Biological Materialism (also known as PASOVACERCEPHHIBIMAT—pronounced "passovah-sayr-seff-HIB-i-mat"). The night following the afternoon of Act One. A table for a desk, an old swivel chair missing a wheel, and a security-system video monitor surveilling an adjoining room in which big glass jars sit in neat rows on shelves. In the jars float human brains. (We see this room only on the video screen.) In the guardroom, Katherina Serafima Gleb, a young woman in her twenties who is wearing the uniform of a security guard, is sitting, staring into space. An old samovar, much less impressive than the samovar in Act One, stands on the table, brewing tea. Popolitipov, wearing a voluminous greatcoat and a big fur hat, covered in snow, bursts in, carrying an ancient, battered guitar case.*)

IPPOLITE IPPOPOLITOVICH POPOLITIPOV
You.

KATHERINA SERAFIMA GLEB

What?

IPPOLITE IPPOPOLITOVICH POPOLITIPOV

Have replaced myself in me.

KATHERINA SERAFIMA GLEB

What?

IPPOLITE IPPOPOLITOVICH POPOLITIPOV

The soul in me that on Judgment Day looked to ascend to bright Heaven has been smitten, obliterated, replaced in me by you.

KATHERINA SERAFIMA GLEB

Too creepy.

IPPOLITE IPPOPOLITOVICH POPOLITIPOV

I am not merely yours, Katherina, I *am* you, I have *become* you.

KATHERINA SERAFIMA GLEB

I said, too creepy.

IPPOLITE IPPOPOLITOVICH POPOLITIPOV

I would like to run my tongue against the salty soft shag covering your upper lip.

KATHERINA SERAFIMA GLEB

Too personal.

IPPOLITE IPPOPOLITOVICH POPOLITIPOV

I want to fuck you.

KATHERINA SERAFIMA GLEB

Don't try anything, Poppy, I'm warning you.

IPPOLITE IPPOPOLITOVICH POPOLITIPOV

Can I sing you a song?

KATHERINA SERAFIMA GLEB

Your voice is repulsive. No. Do you have cigarettes?

IPPOLITE IPPOPOLITOVICH POPOLITIPOV

No. In me there is a yearning, and it complains to me of wanting you, it strains against my skin towards you, it is like the wet lapping of the tide, the pull of the moon on the ocean, like the rise of sap through frozen wood when winter is shattered by the brunt thrust of spring.

KATHERINA SERAFIMA GLEB

Too romantic.

IPPOLITE IPPOPOLITOVICH POPOLITIPOV

Like the hydraulic rush of the river through the dam, the whine of turbines, voltage coursing across a continent of wire.

KATHERINA SERAFIMA GLEB

Too technological.

IPPOLITE IPPOPOLITOVICH POPOLITIPOV

Like the inchoate voluptuous seething of the masses as they surge towards revolutionary consciousness.

KATHERINA SERAFIMA GLEB

(*Overlapping on "surge"*) Too political. Too corny.

IPPOLITE IPPOPOLITOVICH POPOLITIPOV

When I was a child . . .

KATHERINA SERAFIMA GLEB

Too psychological.

IPPOLITE IPPOPOLITOVICH POPOLITIPOV

(*Screams, then*) Give yourself to me, I beg you, Katherina Serafima, or I will blow my brains out I will lie down in a snowbank or under a train or . . .

KATHERINA SERAFIMA GLEB

You were supposed to bring cigarettes, Poppy.

IPPOLITE IPPOPOLITOVICH POPOLITIPOV

I burn my flesh with cigarettes, dreaming of you, I scrape my knuckles along roughcast walls, look, bloody scabs, I deliberately lace my shoes too tight, and cinch my belt till my intestines squirm under pressure, in pain, I refuse myself sleep, dreaming of you, I've slept maybe six, maybe seven hours this whole month, sleep-deprived, trussed and hobbled and why? I mean, are you clever? No. Are you kind? Most certainly not. And yet there is in all your attributes considered and parts taken together a summational, additive kind of perfection: I love you.

KATHERINA SERAFIMA GLEB

You're old.

IPPOLITE IPPOPOLITOVICH POPOLITIPOV

I love you.

KATHERINA SERAFIMA GLEB

I hate you.

IPPOLITE IPPOPOLITOVICH POPOLITIPOV

(*Shouting*) *I LOVE YOU!*

KATHERINA SERAFIMA GLEB

I'm a lesbian.

IPPOLITE IPPOPOLITOVICH POPOLITIPOV

Pervert.

KATHERINA SERAFIMA GLEB

Asshole.

IPPOLITE IPPOPOLITOVICH POPOLITIPOV

Abomination!

KATHERINA SERAFIMA GLEB

Exploiter!

IPPOLITE IPPOPOLITOVICH POPOLITIPOV

Wanton! Abuser!

KATHERINA SERAFIMA GLEB

Harasser! Torturer! *Apparatchik!*

(*He lunges for her. She dodges easily. He falls heavily. She steps on his neck.*)

KATHERINA SERAFIMA GLEB

I warned you.

IPPOLITE IPPOPOLITOVICH POPOLITIPOV
Get off.

KATHERINA SERAFIMA GLEB
Cigarettes.

(He hands them to her. She releases him.)

KATHERINA SERAFIMA GLEB
I'm tired of this, Poppy, I'm going to find an easier way to get a decent smoke. I really am a lesbian, you know. I have a new girlfriend. I'll never have sex with you, I don't want to touch you, and frankly, Poppy, it's not fair you should make me go through this mortifying business over and over and over again, night after night after night; know what? You're a pig.

IPPOLITE IPPOPOLITOVICH POPOLITIPOV
I cannot help myself. *(He begins to remove an ancient guitar from the guitar case.)*

KATHERINA SERAFIMA GLEB
Just because you got me a soft job. A soft, *boring* job. Which I hate. This place is creepy. Know what? At night I hear them slithering.

IPPOLITE IPPOPOLITOVICH POPOLITIPOV
Who?

KATHERINA SERAFIMA GLEB
The brains. They rub their spongy rivules and volutes against the smooth glass sides of their jars. Sometimes they bubble. As if breathing.

IPPOLITE IPPOPOLITOVICH POPOLITIPOV

The brains are dead brains, Katherina.

KATHERINA SERAFIMA GLEB

Then why don't they throw them out?

IPPOLITE IPPOPOLITOVICH POPOLITIPOV

They study them. The great minds of the Party. Political minds. Scientific minds. Even an artist or two.

KATHERINA SERAFIMA GLEB

In my opinion they should throw them out. Most of the older ones are falling apart. No one could make a proper study of them.

Sometimes when I get bored, I grab the jars and shake them up. The brain cells of Vyshinsky. The brain cells of Iron Feliks Dzerzhinsky. Whirl like snowflakes in a crystal snowball.

IPPOLITE IPPOPOLITOVICH POPOLITIPOV

Become my mistress or I will report you.

KATHERINA SERAFIMA GLEB

When you die, Poppy, will they put your brain in a jar?

(Popolitipov begins to play softly, serenading her.)

KATHERINA SERAFIMA GLEB

(Listens to the music a beat, then) Some nights I pretend that I am not simply night watchman but I lead midnight tours through here for insomniac Muscovites whose anxieties or guilty consciences keep them awake. This is my speech:

(*To the audience*) Welcome to The Pan-Soviet Archives for the Study of Cerebro-Cephalognomical Historico-Biological Materialism, also known as PASOVACERCEPHHIBI-MAT. Here the Party has stored the brains of its bygone leaders, an unbroken line of brains stretching back to Red October. Beginning of course with Lenin, most people think his brain is still in his body in the crypt, but it's not, it's here, it is MASSIVE, 1,340 grams of solid brain-flesh, the heaviest brain ever extracted, it's a wonder the poor man could hold his head up his brain was so grotesquely HUGE. Ranked beside it are many other famous brains, all floating in some sort of sudsy lime-green mummifying juice, all the famous Bolshevik brains except for those which got flushed in the notorious dead-brain Purges of 1937. Stalin's brain is here; Brezhnev's, which is dingy-yellow like an old tooth; Andropov's, and now I suppose Chernenko's; he died last week but his brain's not here yet: Maybe they couldn't find it.
(*She goes to Poppy and tousle-pulls his hair.*)
(*Teasingly, torturing him*) Let's talk politics.

IPPOLITE IPPOPOLITOVICH POPOLITIPOV
(*Strumming*) I don't want to talk politics with you, my Katushka, I want to pluck my guitar for you, pick pick pick I pick my heart to pieces.

KATHERINA SERAFIMA GLEB
Gorbachev will replace Chernenko.
Right?
Come on, Poppy. Tell me! Gorbachev will be our honored leader next?
His wife is a Jewess.

IPPOLITE IPPOPOLITOVICH POPOLITIPOV

(Continuing to strum) No she . . .

KATHERINA SERAFIMA GLEB

That's what they say: Jewess.

(Popolitipov continues to play under this.)

KATHERINA SERAFIMA GLEB

I'm not an anti-Semite, I have nothing to do with Jews, but that's what they say.
Tea?

(Popolitipov nods his head "yes," still playing. Katherina goes to the samovar, lifts the lid, reaches within and withdraws an alarmingly large bottle of vodka. She takes a huge swallow and hands it to Popolitipov, who does the same; while he drinks, she hums his tune; and then he starts playing again; throughout all this the music never stops.)

IPPOLITE IPPOPOLITOVICH POPOLITIPOV

Gorbachev isn't a Jew. Nor is Raisa Maxsimovna. She just likes to dress fancy. A strange lust for the sort of pleasures one associates with adolescence seems to have overtaken everyone: panic, mania, nausea, rage. The pleasures of adulthood are forsaken.

KATHERINA SERAFIMA GLEB

What are the pleasures of adulthood?

IPPOLITE IPPOPOLITOVICH POPOLITIPOV

Heartbreak. Agony deep as bone marrow. Quiet, nuanced despair.

(He looks at her. She drinks vodka. He drinks vodka. He plays again.)

KATHERINA SERAFIMA GLEB

Gorbachev will come, trailing free-market anarchy in his wake! Burger King! Pizza Hut! The International Monetary Fund! Billions in aid will flow! Solzhenitsyn will come back from Vermont to thrash and purify us! Kentucky Fried Chicken franchises! Toxic waste! Everything will change then, because Gorbachev is crafty and sly in the manner of Jews. He'll defeat the deadbeat nomenklatura, every last one, including you, Poppy, and then there will be no more politics, we will become like Americans, I will be in a heavy-metal band! There will be *surprises*: most of them unpleasant, but at least unanticipated, and the Great Grey Age of Boredom will finally lift.

(She takes a swig of vodka, he takes a swig of vodka.)

IPPOLITE IPPOPOLITOVICH POPOLITIPOV

To the Great Age of Boredom.

KATHERINA SERAFIMA GLEB

I am inexpressibly, immeasurably sad. Sad sad.

IPPOLITE IPPOPOLITOVICH POPOLITIPOV

Because you are a Slav. Sorrow is the spiritual genius of Slavic peoples.

KATHERINA SERAFIMA GLEB

Bullshit. I don't believe in national identities. Reactionary! I am an anarchist.

IPPOLITE IPPOPOLITOVICH POPOLITIPOV

You are a nihilist.

KATHERINA SERAFIMA GLEB

I am an internationalist. (*Swig of vodka.*)
Like Trotsky! (*Swig of vodka*) The Jew!

(*Pause. He looks at her.*)

IPPOLITE IPPOPOLITOVICH POPOLITIPOV

When I was a child, I was an ugly child, a graceless child,
and did not believe I would be loved and was in fact not
loved by anyone.

KATHERINA SERAFIMA GLEB

Poor Poppy. Poor Poppy the Slav.

IPPOLITE IPPOPOLITOVICH POPOLITIPOV

My mother dead in the Great Patriotic War, in the snow,
German bullet through her spine, her belly, but I was
already a young man by then so it can't have been then
that I lost her love, but earlier, earlier, a point towards
which my memories refuse to travel—I cannot blame
them. My father was a bastard, the Germans got him too.

KATHERINA SERAFIMA GLEB

(*Swigging vodka*) Poppy the orphan.

IPPOLITE IPPOPOLITOVICH POPOLITIPOV

The Party adopted me. The Party was not Love, but
Necessity; it rebuilt the ruined world. Through the Party I
came to love.

KATHERINA SERAFIMA GLEB
Love.

(*Vodka. Sorrow.*)

IPPOLITE IPPOPOLITOVICH POPOLITIPOV
The Party dispenses miracles. The Party drove away the
Czar, immortalized Lenin, withstood France and Britain
and the United States, made Communism in one country,
electrified Russia, milled steel, built railways, abolished
distance, defeated Germany, suspended time, became
Eternal, dispersed the body of each and every member,
molecule by molecule, across an inconceivably vast starry
matrix encompassing the infinite: so that, within the
Party, everything is; so that everything human, even
Marx—was shown as limited and the Party, Illimitable;
and through the illimitable Party the human is exalted,
becomes Divine, occupant of a great chiming spacious-
ness that is not distance but time, time which never
moves nor passes, light which does not travel and yet is
light: And love, pure love, even in a degraded, corrupt
and loveless world, love can finally be born.

(*Little pause, more vodka.*)

IPPOLITE IPPOPOLITOVICH POPOLITIPOV
Do you understand what I am saying to you, Katushka?

KATHERINA SERAFIMA GLEB
(*Softly; deeply moved*) Not a word.

IPPOLITE IPPOPOLITOVICH POPOLITIPOV

(*Very tenderly*) That night, that night, when I saw you that night, I was walking in the Arbat, you had fallen in the snow, sleeping in the gutter, dirty, drunk, rude, radiant: I was overwhelmed with lust, and then followed—love. Love. Love. Love. Love.

(*They are very close; he has almost won.*)

Even in a corrupt and loveless world, love can be born.

(*Katherina leaps to her feet and screams, a long, loud, howl of joy; she rushes across the room at Dr. Bonfila Bezhukhovna Bonch-Bruevich, who is just entering the room, carrying a wrapped parcel, wearing hat and coat, covered in snow. Katherina kisses Bonfila passionately.*)

IPPOLITE IPPOPOLITOVICH POPOLITIPOV

(*Aghast!*) Good GOD!

BONFILA BEZHUKHOVNA BONCH-BRUEVICH

(*Seeing Popolitipov*) Oh my GOD.

KATHERINA SERAFIMA GLEB

GOD I'm happy! (*To Popolitipov*) Hello, Poppy!

BONFILA BEZHUKHOVNA BONCH-BRUEVICH

(*Horror-stricken, bowing her head slightly*) Comrade Commissar, I . . .

KATHERINA SERAFIMA GLEB

See? Lesbians! This is my girlfriend, Doctor Bonf . . .

BONFILA BEZHUKHOVNA BONCH-BRUEVICH
(Cutting her off) I'm interrupting.

(Bonfila turns to leave, Katherina grabs her arm.)

KATHERINA SERAFIMA GLEB
No, Poppy was interrupting, Poppy is always interrupting, but now he's going. Aren't you, Poppy? *(Screaming with rage)* GO, POPPY!!!

BONFILA BEZHUKHOVNA BONCH-BRUEVICH
(To Katherina) You're drunk.

KATHERINA SERAFIMA GLEB
No I'm not.

BONFILA BEZHUKHOVNA BONCH-BRUEVICH
Yes you are!

KATHERINA SERAFIMA GLEB
You're mad at me.
(To Popolitipov) See what you've done.
I need a drink.
(To Popolitipov) See, my sadness is gone, I must not be a true Slav after all. I'm happy you can see her, now maybe you will know that I cannot love you: ever, ever. And she is a physician, she cures people, not an ineffectual aged paperpushing-timeserver-apparatchik-with-a-dacha like you who only bleeds the people dry.

(Awkward pause.)

BONFILA BEZHUKHOVNA BONCH-BRUEVICH

Did I interrupt . . .

(*Pointing to the guitar that Poppy clutches*) Comrade Commissar was playing the . . .

IPPOLITE IPPOPOLITOVICH POPOLITIPOV

(*Putting the guitar away; very, very darkly*) Not anymore. Doctor . . . ?

KATHERINA SERAFIMA GLEB

Bonch-Bruevich!

BONFILA BEZHUKHOVNA BONCH-BRUEVICH

(*Simultaneously*) Comrade Commissar, I . . .

(*To Katherina, hearing that she has said her name*) Shut up.

I'll go.

I'll go.

Somebody should go.

This is mortifying.

IPPOLITE IPPOPOLITOVICH POPOLITIPOV

Is it?

(*Pleasant*) Things change. Some things. We are all liberals.

(*Homicidally angry, to Katherina*) Horseleech! Viper's spawn!

(*Pleasant again*) You are a doctor. Of . . . ?

(*Military command*) Do you have a specialty.

BONFILA BEZHUKHOVNA BONCH-BRUEVICH

Pediatric oncology.

KATHERINA SERAFIMA GLEB

(*Sad*) Kids with cancer.

IPPOLITE IPPOPOLITOVICH POPOLITIPOV

Moscow?

BONFILA BEZHUKHOVNA BONCH-BRUEVICH

I . . . Yes.

IPPOLITE IPPOPOLITOVICH POPOLITIPOV

(*Trying to keep it together but coming unglued*) That's convenient for both of you. You are lucky. Moscow is an agreeable posting, for cosmopolitans such as you and I. Many doctors have to report to places more remote, arctic outposts . . .
(*Little pause; becoming suddenly profoundly sad and weary*) Doctor, may I ask you a health-related question?

BONFILA BEZHUKHOVNA BONCH-BRUEVICH

Certainly.

IPPOLITE IPPOPOLITOVICH POPOLITIPOV

(*In confidence, in earnest*) If a man were to shoot himself, against which of the various customary vulnerable points of the body would you advise he position the barrel of his gun?

BONFILA BEZHUKHOVNA BONCH-BRUEVICH

I . . .

IPPOLITE IPPOPOLITOVICH POPOLITIPOV

Temple? Soft palate? Heart?

KATHERINA SERAFIMA GLEB

I have a friend who died by shooting himself in the armpit. The bullet went through his shoulder and into his nose.

(*Katherina bursts into gales of drunken laughter.*
A beat; Bonfila and Popolitipov stare at Katherina.)

BONFILA BEZHUKHOVNA BONCH-BRUEVICH
(*Softly, deferentially*) I would advise him not to shoot himself, Comrade Commissar. I would advise him to live.

IPPOLITE IPPOPOLITOVICH POPOLITIPOV
Say his life had become unbearable.

BONFILA BEZHUKHOVNA BONCH-BRUEVICH
Life is almost never literally unbearable. We choose whether or not we bear up. We choose.

IPPOLITE IPPOPOLITOVICH POPOLITIPOV
Circumstances may dictate otherwise. History.

BONFILA BEZHUKHOVNA BONCH-BRUEVICH
People make their own history.

IPPOLITE IPPOPOLITOVICH POPOLITIPOV
Limits are set by the conditions of their social development.

KATHERINA SERAFIMA GLEB
(*By rote, a thing she learned in school*) Those conditions are themselves affected by the state of their economic relations.

(*Pause. The others look at Katherina.*)

KATHERINA SERAFIMA GLEB
Which in turn are related to a particular stage of the mode of production.

(*She sits heavily, slumps over, falls asleep.*)

IPPOLITE IPPOPOLITOVICH POPOLITIPOV
(*Crossing to the sleeping Kat; he looks at her, then*) Her head is stuffed full of pottery shards, rags, ash and wind. She is the Revolution's Great-Granddaughter. She is . . . a barbarian.

BONFILA BEZHUKHOVNA BONCH-BRUEVICH
She's immature. And can't drink.
And I think she doesn't like you very much.

IPPOLITE IPPOPOLITOVICH POPOLITIPOV
I must be going.

KATHERINA SERAFIMA GLEB
(*Still slumped over, drowsy*) Try the armpit, Poppy.

IPPOLITE IPPOPOLITOVICH POPOLITIPOV
(*A beat; then, bracing himself for the mortal blow*) If I shoot myself, Katherina, will you miss me?

KATHERINA SERAFIMA GLEB
(*Looking up*) Maybe. For a day or two. Maybe.
The cigarettes, definitely.
Not really. No.
Oh Poppy, I'm sorry, but you're a pig, you know, and I would like to be kind, but I can't. (*She sleeps.*)

IPPOLITE IPPOPOLITOVICH POPOLITIPOV
We have not made kind people.

(*To Bonfila, not without menace*) We have not made a world that makes people kind.
(*He leaves.*)

BONFILA BEZHUKHOVNA BONCH-BRUEVICH
Is he really going to shoot himself?

(*Katherina snores, loudly.*)

SCENE 2

(*The guardroom. Several hours later. Katherina and Bonfila sit at the table, both drunk, Katherina more drunk; the parcel, still wrapped, is on the table between them. Also on the table is a now nearly empty bottle of vodka.*)

BONFILA BEZHUKHOVNA BONCH-BRUEVICH
My great-grandfather was Vladimir Dimitrievich Bonch-Bruevich. Do you know who that is?

(*Katherina shakes her head "no."*)

BONFILA BEZHUKHOVNA BONCH-BRUEVICH
First Secretary of the Sovnarkom.
The Council of People's Commissars. 1918. A founder of the Party.

KATHERINA SERAFIMA GLEB
Never heard of him.

BONFILA BEZHUKHOVNA BONCH-BRUEVICH
It's your history.

Slavs!

KATHERINA SERAFIMA GLEB

I have no history. What's in the package?

BONFILA BEZHUKHOVNA BONCH-BRUEVICH

My great-grandfather is the man who embalmed Lenin.
He selected the design for the tomb.

KATHERINA SERAFIMA GLEB

You're angry with me because I'm drunk.

BONFILA BEZHUKHOVNA BONCH-BRUEVICH

Not as angry as I was when I was sober.

KATHERINA SERAFIMA GLEB

Promise we'll be lovers forever.

BONFILA BEZHUKHOVNA BONCH-BRUEVICH

No.

KATHERINA SERAFIMA GLEB

Promise we'll be lovers till I'm sober.

BONFILA BEZHUKHOVNA BONCH-BRUEVICH

Yes.

KATHERINA SERAFIMA GLEB

If you leave me I'll kill you.

BONFILA BEZHUKHOVNA BONCH-BRUEVICH

Oh bullshit.

KATHERINA SERAFIMA GLEB

Is Poppy dead yet, do you think?

You've been my lover for more than a month, and look, you still visit me late at night, you bring me mysterious packages . . .

BONFILA BEZHUKHOVNA BONCH-BRUEVICH

Three weeks, it's only been . . . It's still new to me, all this . . .

KATHERINA SERAFIMA GLEB

You won't leave me, will you?

BONFILA BEZHUKHOVNA BONCH-BRUEVICH

I love you.

KATHERINA SERAFIMA GLEB

That's not what I asked. Everyone loves me, but I'm unbearable.

I need someone who will . . . stay, or . . .

I'm sad again.

BONFILA BEZHUKHOVNA BONCH-BRUEVICH

My great-grandfather was also a great Slavophile, a folklorist.

KATHERINA SERAFIMA GLEB

Sadness is the spiritual genius of the Slavic peoples.

BONFILA BEZHUKHOVNA BONCH-BRUEVICH

Uh-huh.

He wrote that the revolts of the Old Believers against Peter the Great were early stirrings of the Revolution among the peoples.

KATHERINA SERAFIMA GLEB

Peter the Great, 1672–1725.

BONFILA BEZHUKHOVNA BONCH-BRUEVICH

My great-grandfather also collected icons. And he planned the Lenin Cult.

KATHERINA SERAFIMA GLEB

Lenin: 1870–1923.

BONFILA BEZHUKHOVNA BONCH-BRUEVICH

1924. When Lenin died, peasants from Tsarskoe Selo sent this to my great-grandpa, to put in the tomb.

(She unwraps the package. It's an old icon, with a metal candleholder attached, in which is a red glass, inside of which is a candle.)

BONFILA BEZHUKHOVNA BONCH-BRUEVICH

See? It's Lenin. They painted his face over an icon of St. Sergius of Radonezh, who lived six hundred years ago . . .

(Little pause. Katherina drinks most of the rest of the vodka, passes the last swallow to Bonfila, who drinks it.)

BONFILA BEZHUKHOVNA BONCH-BRUEVICH

. . . and who is said to have been a great worker of miracles.

KATHERINA SERAFIMA GLEB
We need more vodka.

BONFILA BEZHUKHOVNA BONCH-BRUEVICH
There is no more vodka.

KATHERINA SERAFIMA GLEB
We must go out and get some more vodka.

BONFILA BEZHUKHOVNA BONCH-BRUEVICH
It's too late. It must be four A.M. There won't be a store open.

KATHERINA SERAFIMA GLEB
Why won't you make love to me?

BONFILA BEZHUKHOVNA BONCH-BRUEVICH
Here?

KATHERINA SERAFIMA GLEB
Oh who gives a fuck where? Sure, here. If you love me what would it matter.

BONFILA BEZHUKHOVNA BONCH-BRUEVICH
Too creepy.

KATHERINA SERAFIMA GLEB
Do it, here. Put your hand down my coveralls, slip it deep inside me, blow hot fog-breath in my ears till my brains cook, let me lick your cunt till my whole face is wet, put my hair in your mouth, nip my buttocks, let me scream joyfully as if a hungry animal I want to feed is eating me up!

BONFILA BEZHUKHOVNA BONCH-BRUEVICH
You embarrass me.

KATHERINA SERAFIMA GLEB
You're afraid of sex with me.

BONFILA BEZHUKHOVNA BONCH-BRUEVICH
Nonsense.

(Little pause.)

I'm afraid of sex with you in front of a Deputy Secretary of . . .

KATHERINA SERAFIMA GLEB
He's off shooting himself.
We're alone. I still have all my clothes on. Something's wrong.

BONFILA BEZHUKHOVNA BONCH-BRUEVICH
He won't shoot himself, and tomorrow he'll have us both arrested. Ten years in an institution!

KATHERINA SERAFIMA GLEB
Under Gorbachev people will not be . . .

BONFILA BEZHUKHOVNA BONCH-BRUEVICH
(Overlap) Or maybe he'll have me transferred, just me, alone, to some godforsaken town in Uzbekistan; it was very, very, very stupid of you to kiss me like that in the open like that, to . . .

KATHERINA SERAFIMA GLEB

He's probably dead by now—Poppy—and anyway he
wouldn't . . .

BONFILA BEZHUKHOVNA BONCH-BRUEVICH

(*Overlap, continuous from above*) . . . to draw down atten-
tion like that, to *deliberately* . . .
HOW THE HELL DO YOU KNOW WHAT HE'D . . .
You're ignorant. You don't know anything.

(*Pause.*)

KATHERINA SERAFIMA GLEB

St. Sergius of Radonezh. 1314–1392.
You're yelling because you're afraid of me.

BONFILA BEZHUKHOVNA BONCH-BRUEVICH

Yes.

(*They kiss. It gets hot, then hotter, then cold.*)

BONFILA BEZHUKHOVNA BONCH-BRUEVICH

Sexual deviance is symptomatic of cultures of luxury, in
which monied classes cultivate morbid fascinations with
biological functions, especially sex, tending towards nar-
cissistic, antisocial, unproductive behavior such as . . .
Anyway I don't believe in lesbians, I believe in the working class as the only repository for real historical agency.
You're right I am afraid of you.

KATHERINA SERAFIMA GLEB

Why did you come?

BONFILA BEZHUKHOVNA BONCH-BRUEVICH
To show you this. (*The icon.*)
My great-grandmother is dying. She's one hundred and five
years old. Endurance is the spiritual genius of Slavic peoples.
She gave me this. She says it still works miracles.

KATHERINA SERAFIMA GLEB
Who do you pray to when you light the candle, Lenin or
St. Sergius?

BONFILA BEZHUKHOVNA BONCH-BRUEVICH
She didn't say.

KATHERINA SERAFIMA GLEB
What miracles has it worked?

BONFILA BEZHUKHOVNA BONCH-BRUEVICH
She didn't say that either.

KATHERINA SERAFIMA GLEB
Let's pray for vodka.

BONFILA BEZHUKHOVNA BONCH-BRUEVICH
Shouldn't it be for something less frivolous?

KATHERINA SERAFIMA GLEB
I pray for you to love me enough to be true to your
promise.

BONFILA BEZHUKHOVNA BONCH-BRUEVICH
What promise.

KATHERINA SERAFIMA GLEB

That you'll never leave me.

BONFILA BEZHUKHOVNA BONCH-BRUEVICH

Till you're sober.

KATHERINA SERAFIMA GLEB

(*Very serious*) Then I must never be sober again.
Let's pray for vodka.

BONFILA BEZHUKHOVNA BONCH-BRUEVICH

Match.

(*Katherina gives her one. Bonfila lights the candle. The room darkens. Katherina kneels, bows her head.*)

KATHERINA SERAFIMA GLEB

St. Lenin or St. Sergius, whoever you are. Please hear the prayer of your little daughter. Look down on her from heaven, she's in the room of dead brains; send vodka. So that I may stay pathetically drunk so that she will never leave me, because I'm full of violence and self-pity and lies, but I do have decent feelings too, and dreams that are beautiful, that I'm not ashamed of having, and there was no earthly thing I could attach them to until I made her love me. Please help me little father. Please hear my prayer.

(*Pause.
A big babushka enters, covered in snow.*)

BIG BABUSHKA

(*No pauses*) Kat, I'll tell you what, I was sweeping the snow off the steps up front and along comes this huge truckload of soldiers plowing down the street, sliding on the ice and bang it smacks into a telephone pole and goes over on its side and all the soldiers come tumbling out, and I rush over to see was anyone hurt, and someone was because a soldier's running up and down the street spattering blood in the snow and we can't get him to stop because naturally they're all drunken idiots from the sticks and he's screaming "I'm dying, I'm dying, mother, mother," and all the yelling frightens a dog who bites a cop who swings a club which smashes a big store window; dog, glass, blood, soldiers, and finally we got the boy calmed down and sent him off wrapped up in a bandage and the dog's run off and the cop sees it's a liquor store window he's smashed so he gives me a big bottle of this vodka to shut me up about it (because everyone knows my mouth) which I can't drink because my liver's already the size of my head and so here, I've brought it to you, you drunken slut, because I'm fond of you as if you were my own granddaughter, now I got to go finish sweeping the snow before more falls. (*The big babushka slams a big bottle of vodka down on the table. She squints at the icon*) St. Sergius of Radonezh with the face of Great Lenin.

(*She crosses herself and exits.*
Katherina and Bonfila look at the vodka, and each other, agape.)

SCENE 3

(Even later. Katherina is asleep with her head in Bonfila's lap. Bonfila strokes Katherina's hair and looks at the icon, before which the candle is still burning. The second bottle of vodka stands, almost empty, beside the first empty bottle.)

BONFILA BEZHUKHOVNA BONCH-BRUEVICH
(Very softly) Little father:
You left us alone and see the state we've fallen into? Shouldn't you come back to us now? We have suffered and suffered and Paradise has not arrived. Shouldn't you come back and tell us what went wrong?
She says your brain is in a jar next door: Your body is across town. Pull yourself together, leave your tomb, come claim your brain, remember speech, and action, and once more, having surveyed the wreckage we have made, tell your children: What is to be done?
Shouldn't you come back now?

(Little red candle lights blink on everywhere.)

BONFILA BEZHUKHOVNA BONCH-BRUEVICH
(Like on Christmas morning) Kat. Wake up. Kat. Wake up. Katherina.

KATHERINA SERAFIMA GLEB
What?

BONFILA BEZHUKHOVNA BONCH-BRUEVICH
(Looking about at the lights, wonderingly) Do you . . .

KATHERINA SERAFIMA GLEB

(Asleep) What is it?

BONFILA BEZHUKHOVNA BONCH-BRUEVICH

(Standing) Do you see? Do you see? It's . . .

(A little girl, dressed in a skirt and pullover sweater, enters, and silently looks at Bonfila.
Bonfila screams.
Katherina stands up abruptly.)

KATHERINA SERAFIMA GLEB

(Terrified, blind) I drank too much. Much too much. I've blinded myself. *(She gropes about for Bonfila)* B! B! Don't leave me! Don't leave me!
The lights are going out.

(The lights go out.)

ACT THREE

I'm hanging on to the tram strap
of these terrible times,
and I don't know why I'm alive.

—OSIP MANDELSTAM
The Moscow Notebooks
(Translated by Richard and
Elizabeth McKane)

SCENE 1

(Talmenka, Siberia; 1992. A white room in a medical facility. The little girl who appeared at the end of Act Two, Vodya Domik, is now sitting in a wooden chair. She is expressionless, and mostly very still, although she blinks and occasionally, though infrequently, scratches her arm or shifts in the chair. She sits alone for a few beats. Yegor Tremens Rodent enters, wearing hat, coat, mittens, muffler, umbrella, galoshes; he's carrying a cheap overstuffed briefcase. He is, as always, timorous and deferential, but in the intervening years he's gotten nasty. He tries to hide this; as the scene progresses it emerges.

An old samovar stands in the corner, dead cold. Near it a kettle on a hotplate.

Rodent looks at Vodya, who stares ahead. Several beats pass.)

YEGOR TREMENS RODENT

Hello little girl.

(Vodya has no reaction whatsoever, and has none throughout what follows. Rodent's tone is maddeningly unvaried:

mild, cheerful, each attempt exactly the same as the one preceding, rather like a parrot.)

YEGOR TREMENS RODENT

Hello little girl.
Hello little girl.
Hello.
Hello.
Hello little girl.
Hello little girl.
Hello little girl.
Hello. Hello. Hello. Little girl.

(Pause. He thinks, then:)

Hello little girl.
Hello little girl.
Hello little girl. *(Getting a little ratty-panicky.)*
Hello. Hello. Hello little girl. Little girl.
    Little girl.
    Little . . .

*(He pauses again to look around and to think.
Bonfila comes in, looking different—older, more tired—than in the previous act. Rodent doesn't hear her come in.)*

YEGOR TREMENS RODENT

Hello little girl.
Hello little girl.
Hello little girl.

BONFILA BEZHUKHOVNA BONCH-BRUEVICH

She doesn't . . .

YEGOR TREMENS RODENT

(*Badly frightened*) OH!!

BONFILA BEZHUKHOVNA BONCH-BRUEVICH

She doesn't speak. Deputy Councilor Rodent?

YEGOR TREMENS RODENT

(*Shaken, nervous*) Assistant Deputy Councilor.
Rodent, um, yes.
(*Inclining his head towards Vodya*) She . . . is . . . Mute?
Deaf-mute, or . . . ?

(*Bonfila shrugs.*)

BONFILA BEZHUKHOVNA BONCH-BRUEVICH

Welcome to Talmenka.

(*She exits. Rodent looks at the door through which she has
exited, then turns back to Vodya, looks at her for a minute
and then, exactly as before:*)

YEGOR TREMENS RODENT

Hello little girl.
Hello little girl.
Hello little girl.
Hello little girl.
Want a boiled sweet?
(*Mildly malicious*) No, I don't have any boiled sweets.
Hello little girl.

Hello little girl.
Hello little . . .

(Mrs. Shastlivyi Domik, Vodya's mother, enters abruptly; she is dressed pretty much like a young babushka. She isn't loud but every word she speaks is a bullet aimed at the person she's addressing. Rodent spins to face her.)

MRS. SHASTLIVYI DOMIK

Her name is Vodya. Domik.

YEGOR TREMENS RODENT

Why doesn't she . . .

MRS. SHASTLIVYI DOMIK

She doesn't.

(Mrs. Domik exits abruptly. Rodent looks at Vodya. A beat, then:)

YEGOR TREMENS RODENT

Hello little girl.
Hello little. . .

(Bonfila and Mrs. Domik enter together.)

BONFILA BEZHUKHOVNA BONCH-BRUEVICH

Assistant Deputy Councilor Y. T. Rodent, this is Mrs. Shastlivyi Domik, the child's mother.

MRS. SHASTLIVYI DOMIK

Her name is Vodya.

BONFILA BEZHUKHOVNA BONCH-BRUEVICH
Assistant Deputy Councilor Rodent has come from Moscow. He's come to make a report to President Yeltsin.

YEGOR TREMENS RODENT
(*Nervous little laugh, then*) Well, not *directly* to . . .

BONFILA BEZHUKHOVNA BONCH-BRUEVICH
(*Overlap*) He's come to see what's going on here. About the children.

(*They all look at Vodya.*)

YEGOR TREMENS RODENT
(*Official, but still nervous*) Can she hear what we say?

BONFILA BEZHUKHOVNA BONCH-BRUEVICH
Probably.

YEGOR TREMENS RODENT
But she doesn't speak.

BONFILA BEZHUKHOVNA BONCH-BRUEVICH
No.

YEGOR TREMENS RODENT
Can she, I mean is she . . .

BONFILA BEZHUKHOVNA BONCH-BRUEVICH
Theoretically, yes, I mean she's *able*, she has a larynx, a tongue, she . . . So theoretically, yes but . . .

MRS. SHASTLIVYI DOMIK

(Overlapping on second "theoretically") She doesn't speak.
She never speaks.

YEGOR TREMENS RODENT

How old is she.

BONCH-BRUEVICH AND DOMIK

(Together) Eight.

(Pause.)

YEGOR TREMENS RODENT

I . . .

(Nervous laugh.)

Well how horrible.

(Pause.)

BONFILA BEZHUKHOVNA BONCH-BRUEVICH

Several of the children have died before their sixth birthday. She's the oldest. She's our survivor.

YEGOR TREMENS RODENT

I thought . . . um, I was told she'd be, um, um, um, yellow.

BONFILA BEZHUKHOVNA BONCH-BRUEVICH

They're all yellow at birth, we have no idea why, really,
but. That's why they're called Yellow Children. The jaun-
dice fades by their first birthday.

The older they get the more we see it. Nervous-system damage, renal malformation, liver, cataracts at three, bone-marrow problems.

YEGOR TREMENS RODENT

See what?

BONFILA BEZHUKHOVNA BONCH-BRUEVICH

What?

YEGOR TREMENS RODENT

You said, "the more we see *it*." What is "it"?

BONFILA BEZHUKHOVNA BONCH-BRUEVICH

(*A beat, then a bit more assertive, confrontational*) They mostly don't walk until . . . How old was Vodya?

MRS. SHASTLIVYI DOMIK

Four.

BONFILA BEZHUKHOVNA BONCH-BRUEVICH

And they don't speak. A few have words, minimal speech, she doesn't.
We've ruled out pretty much everything you'd normally look for: pesticides, industrial pollutants, something the parents are eating. They eat badly here but . . .

MRS. SHASTLIVYI DOMIK

We've always eaten badly.

(*Little pause.*)

YEGOR TREMENS RODENT

So it isn't the diet.

MRS. SHASTLIVYI DOMIK

We've always eaten badly.

BONFILA BEZHUKHOVNA BONCH-BRUEVICH

It's genetic. Inherited. Probably chromosome alteration due to her parents' exposure to ionizing radiation.
Or her parents' parents. In significantly high doses, wave, not particulate, not on the ground or on food, but from a . . .
In 1949, two hundred and fifty miles from here, in Kazakhstan, in the Semipalatinsk area, the army detonated a nuclear warhead. They detonated the warhead to put out a minor oil fire. An experiment. No one of course was evacuated.

YEGOR TREMENS RODENT

(*Shrugs sadly*) Stalin.

BONFILA BEZHUKHOVNA BONCH-BRUEVICH

(*Even more aggressive*) The place I worked in last year, Chelyabinsk, there's a cave, full of something in leaky barrels. Unmarked railway cars used to pass through the town late at night, smoking, on their way to the cave, you could smell the fumes everywhere. Not Stalin. Last year.

YEGOR TREMENS RODENT

It's a storage facility.

BONFILA BEZHUKHOVNA BONCH-BRUEVICH

So, basically, you ask what's wrong with her. Well, in my opinion and in the opinion of my colleagues, she's a mutation. A nuclear mutant. Third generation. She has a sister who's "healthy"; I wonder what *her* children will be like?

YEGOR TREMENS RODENT

(*To Mrs. Domik*) I'm sorry.

(*Mrs. Domik walks out.*)

BONFILA BEZHUKHOVNA BONCH-BRUEVICH

In Altograd, which is where I was before I was in Chelyabinsk, there's twenty times the normal rate for thyroid cancer. There's a lake full of blind fish. Everyone has nosebleeds. Everyone's chronically fatigued. Leukemia is epidemic. The reactor plant near there has cracks in the casing, steam comes through several times a month, it's the same kind as at Chernobyl, it was supposed to be closed, it isn't, and the caves in Chelyabinsk? The stuff you have in there, probably cesium, strontium, certainly bomb-grade plutonium, piled up since when? 1950? It's seeping into the aquifer; sixty feet per year. Do you know what that means? There's a river nearby. Millions drink from it. This is documented. The Dnieper's already shot from Chernobyl, and people still drink from that. Millions. The plutonium in that cave. Three hundred pounds of it could kill every person on the planet. You have thirty *tons* down there, in rusting drums. The people of Altograd voted for you to move it, a referendum, last year: Why? Why hasn't it been moved?

YEGOR TREMENS RODENT

To where?

BONFILA BEZHUKHOVNA BONCH-BRUEVICH

The whole country's a radioactive swamp, waste dumps, warheads, malfunctioning reactors, there are six hundred nuclear waste sites in *Moscow*, for God's sake. Hundreds upon hundreds of thousands of people have been exposed.

(Little pause.)

YEGOR TREMENS RODENT

The world has changed with an unimaginable rapidity. People grow impatient. Everything is new now, and everything is terrible. In the old days I would not have been forced to do this sort of work.

(With a little menace) In the old days you would not speak to me like this.

(Little pause.)

BONFILA BEZHUKHOVNA BONCH-BRUEVICH

All I ever see are the regional authorities, and they're just the same old Party bosses who just . . .

YEGOR TREMENS RODENT

(Official) But you see, doctor, there's nothing to be done. We have no place to put it. We used to dump it into the sea, the . . . That's frowned on by the International Community, it's understandable, they'll take away our loans if we . . . We have no money. Trillions. It would cost trillions. And some of these places will simply never be

inhabitable again. Regardless of the money. Twenty thousand years.

(*Mrs. Domik slams back into the room, stands glowering.*)

YEGOR TREMENS RODENT
And anyway, we're broke.

BONFILA BEZHUKHOVNA BONCH-BRUEVICH
And now you're offering to process and store radioactive and toxic waste from the West.

YEGOR TREMENS RODENT
(*Overlap*) They'll pay us.

BONFILA BEZHUKHOVNA BONCH-BRUEVICH
(*Overlap*) But store it where?

YEGOR TREMENS RODENT
(*Overlap*) We need the money. The Russian People need the . . .

BONFILA BEZHUKHOVNA BONCH-BRUEVICH
(*Overlap*) You've conducted tests. On uninformed citizens. Whole populations, the Russian People . . .

YEGOR TREMENS RODENT
(*Overlap, snide*) I, personally, never did that.

BONFILA BEZHUKHOVNA BONCH-BRUEVICH
(*Overlap*) The West doesn't do that. Expose its citizens unknowingly to radiation, to . . . Even the United States would never do that.

YEGOR TREMENS RODENT

Oh don't be so certain . . .

BONFILA BEZHUKHOVNA BONCH-BRUEVICH

I am . . . certain, the Western democracies, even capitalist countries don't . . .

YEGOR TREMENS RODENT

(*Overlap*) Then move to the West. Anyone can, now. If they'll let you in. Which of course they won't. What do you want from me?

BONFILA BEZHUKHOVNA BONCH-BRUEVICH

I want to know.

YEGOR TREMENS RODENT

What?

BONFILA BEZHUKHOVNA BONCH-BRUEVICH

BECAUSE I AM . . . *STILL*, A SOCIALIST! Isn't that absurd! After all I've seen I still believe . . . And, and I want to know! And you, SOMEONE MUST TELL ME! How this . . . How this came to pass. How any of this came to pass. In a socialist country. In the world's first socialist country.

(*Little pause.*)

YEGOR TREMENS RODENT

Naïveté.

BONFILA BEZHUKHOVNA BONCH-BRUEVICH

It's the spiritual genius of Slavic peoples.

YEGOR TREMENS RODENT

(*A brief pause; trying to figure her out, now he's got the upper hand*) What are you doing in Siberia.

BONFILA BEZHUKHOVNA BONCH-BRUEVICH

I was transferred by the Ministry of Health Services in 1985.

YEGOR TREMENS RODENT

You must have made someone angry.

BONFILA BEZHUKHOVNA BONCH-BRUEVICH

As a matter of fact I did. Not angry, jealous. He had me transferred.

YEGOR TREMENS RODENT

But things are different now. You could go back.

BONFILA BEZHUKHOVNA BONCH-BRUEVICH

Yes.

YEGOR TREMENS RODENT

In fact, you could have gone back there five years ago, in 1987 you could have gone back. (*With mock enthusiasm*) Perestroika!

BONFILA BEZHUKHOVNA BONCH-BRUEVICH

I suppose so. I was afraid.

YEGOR TREMENS RODENT

Of the man who had you transferred?

BONFILA BEZHUKHOVNA BONCH-BRUEVICH

No.

Someone I disappointed. I disappointed a friend, I hurt her, badly, and I was afraid to face her again. So I stayed here. Why are you asking me . . . ?

YEGOR TREMENS RODENT

(*Shrug, nasty smile*) The Steppes, the Taiga, it's an unhealthy place. Siberia, doctor, is making you shrill.

MRS. SHASTLIVYI DOMIK

(*Suddenly, to Rodent, very upset*) Compensation. Money. You're from Moscow, do you understand me?

YEGOR TREMENS RODENT

Yes, I understand what comp . . .

MRS. SHASTLIVYI DOMIK

(*Continuous from above, and throughout this section she runs right over what Rodent says, taking only little breaths when he begins to speak*) I want to be compensated. Look at her. Look. She'll never be anything.

YEGOR TREMENS RODENT

I'm truly sorry about your . . .

MRS. SHASTLIVYI DOMIK

(*Overlap*) I will need to be compensated. Look. Look. What am I supposed to do with . . .

YEGOR TREMENS RODENT

I have forms for you to fill out and . . .

MRS. SHASTLIVYI DOMIK

(*Overlap*) How am I supposed to feed her? You cut back on my assistance . . .

YEGOR TREMENS RODENT

It's very hard all over Russia, Mrs. . .

MRS. SHASTLIVYI DOMIK

(*Overlap*) I can't live without my assistance and you took most of it, it's a pittance, how am I supposed to feed her, she eats, and watch her, she has to be watched every second and you closed down the day hospital, you cut assistance so compensate me. And medicine, now I have to pay for medicine, more than half the money we have goes for . . .

YEGOR TREMENS RODENT

Austerity measures are necessary to . . . Doctor, can you get her to . . .

MRS. SHASTLIVYI DOMIK

(*Overlap*) . . . for medicine, and how do I pay for that medicine is expensive when I can't work because what work is there that *pays*, that really *pays*, and with *inflation* . . .

YEGOR TREMENS RODENT

The transition to a free-market economy requires sacrifice.

MRS. SHASTLIVYI DOMIK

(*Overlap*) . . . my God, inflation, money's worthless and who has what you need for the black market, it's impossible, I should be compensated and . . .

YEGOR TREMENS RODENT

The World Bank is promising . . .

BONFILA BEZHUKHOVNA BONCH-BRUEVICH

(Simultaneous with Rodent) Mrs. Domik, I think you should maybe sit and I'll get some tea . . .

MRS. SHASTLIVYI DOMIK

(Overlap) . . . and anyway who'll mind her if I work. *(To Bonfila)* I DON'T WANT TEA, and what have you ever done for her, huh, except tests and tests and tests, you haven't helped any of the children, and she's not dying she's *growing*, and who's supposed to mind her if I have to work all day, she doesn't just sit now, she wanders, across roads, and . . . Well? WHAT ABOUT MY DAUGHTER? WHAT ABOUT MY DAUGHTER? WHAT ARE YOU GOING TO DO ABOUT MY DAUGHTER? WHO'LL PAY FOR THAT?

BONFILA BEZHUKHOVNA BONCH-BRUEVICH

Please, Mrs. Domik, there are other patients in the . . .

MRS. SHASTLIVYI DOMIK

Take her!

(Mrs. Domik yanks Vodya out of the chair and drags her over to Rodent, who recoils with fear. Mrs. Domik shoves the child against Rodent.)

MRS. SHASTLIVYI DOMIK

She's not a, a, a person! NO! Take her to Yeltsin! Take her to Gorbachev! Take her to Gaidar! Take her to Clinton!

YOU care for her! YOU did this! YOU did this! She's YOURS.

(*Mrs. Domik exits.*
Bonfila takes Vodya and leads her back to her chair.)

YEGOR TREMENS RODENT
Um, um, um . . .

(*Bonfila goes out of the room.*
Rodent goes over to Vodya and pats her on the head.
Mrs. Domik comes back in, alone, wearing a coat and scarf, and carrying the same for Vodya.)

MRS. SHASTLIVYI DOMIK
Get your filthy fucking hands off my child.

(*Rodent moves away from Vodya, sits. Mrs. Domik bundles Vodya up, preparing to leave.*)

YEGOR TREMENS RODENT
(*Quietly, carefully, furtively*) Mrs. Domik, may I speak to you, not as a representative of the government but in confidence, as one Russian to another?
(*Little pause.*)
This nation is falling apart. It is in the hands of miscreants and fools. The government does not serve the people, but betrays the people to foreign interests. The tragedy of your daughter is but one instance, a tragic instance of the continuance of the crimes of the Communist era through to the present day. Chaos threatens. The land is poisoned. The United States is becoming

our landlord. Dark-skinned people from the Caucasus regions, Muslims, Asiatics, swarthy inferior races have flooded Moscow, and white Christian Russians such as you and I are expected to support them. There is no order and no strength; the army is bound hand and foot by foreign agents pretending to be our leaders, but they are not our leaders. They stand idly by as the United Nations imposes sanctions and threatens war against our brother Slavs in Serbia who are fighting to liberate Bosnia; the great Pan-Slavic Empire has been stolen from us again by the International Jew. Not because we are weak: We have enormous bombs, chemicals, secret weapons. Because we lack a leader, a man of iron and will; but the leader is coming, Mrs. Domik, already he is here, already I and millions like us who have joined the Liberal Democratic Party of Russia support him. We need more women. Motherland Mrs. Domik is the spiritual genius of Slavic peoples.

(Reaching in his briefcase) Would you like some literature?

(He proffers a pamphlet; Mrs. Domik takes it, looks it over as if examining a rotten piece of fruit; she fixes Rodent with a look, smiling in an ugly way; then crumples his pamphlet and drops it on the floor.)

MRS. SHASTLIVYI DOMIK

(Smiling) Listen, you fucking ferret, I'm not a fucking "Russian like you," I'm a Lithuanian, and I fucking hate Russians; and why am I here in Siberia, because fucking Stalin sent my grandma here fifty years ago. My grandpa and my great-uncles and great-aunts died tunneling

through the Urals on chain gangs. Their father and his brother were shot in Vilnius, their children were shot fighting Germans, my sister starved to death and my brother killed himself under fucking Brezhnev after fifteen years in a psychiatric hospital, I've tried twice to do the same—and my *daughter* . . .

Fuck this century. Fuck your leader. Fuck the state. Fuck all governments, fuck the motherland, fuck your mother, your father and you.

(Mrs. Domik takes Vodya's hand and exits.
Rodent, ashen with terror, puts his literature back in his briefcase, stands, begins to put his coat and gear on.
Bonfila enters.)

BONFILA BEZHUKHOVNA BONCH-BRUEVICH
Leaving?

YEGOR TREMENS RODENT
Mm-hmm.

BONFILA BEZHUKHOVNA BONCH-BRUEVICH
Would you like to meet more of the children?

YEGOR TREMENS RODENT
Er, um, no, no, not necessary.

BONFILA BEZHUKHOVNA BONCH-BRUEVICH
We could go through files . . .

YEGOR TREMENS RODENT
Send them to my office, send them to Moscow.
(Little pause.)

BONFILA BEZHUKHOVNA BONCH-BRUEVICH

I also didn't go back to Moscow . . . You know when you asked me earlier? Why didn't I go back? Because I thought I could do some good here. In the face of all this impossibility, twenty thousand years, that little girl who won't live five more years, I still believe that good can be done, that there's work to be done. Good hard work.

YEGOR TREMENS RODENT

(*A little smile*) To the Motherland. To the work ahead. Goodbye.

(*He exits.*
Bonfila is alone for a beat.
She kicks the little chair in which Vodya had been sitting, sending it clattering across the room.
Another brief beat, and then Katherina enters, dressed in a medical assistant's coat.)

KATHERINA SERAFIMA GLEB

I'm dying for a smoke. Did you remember the cigarettes?

(*Bonfila takes a pack of cigarettes out of her labcoat pocket, and gives them to Katherina.*)

BONFILA BEZHUKHOVNA BONCH-BRUEVICH

They're bad for your health.

KATHERINA SERAFIMA GLEB

Yeah, yeah. To Moscow. I want to go to Moscow.

BONFILA BEZHUKHOVNA BONCH-BRUEVICH

You say that every single day.

KATHERINA SERAFIMA GLEB

Some day you'll say yes.

BONFILA BEZHUKHOVNA BONCH-BRUEVICH

Are you sorry you followed me here?

KATHERINA SERAFIMA GLEB

I didn't follow you, you *begged* me to come.
Siberia sucks.
I'm done for the day. Are you ready for home?

BONFILA BEZHUKHOVNA BONCH-BRUEVICH

I'm ready.

EPILOGUE

▼

Are the democracies that govern the world's richest countries capable of solving the problems that communism has failed to solve? That is the question. Historical communism has failed, I don't deny it. But the problems remain—those same problems which the communist utopia pointed out and held to be solvable, and which now exist, or very soon will, on a world scale. That is why one would be foolish to rejoice at the defeat and to rub one's hands saying: "We always said so!" Do people really think that the end of historical communism (I stress the word "historical") has put an end to poverty and the thirst for justice? In our world the two-thirds society rules and prospers without having anything to fear from the third of poor devils. But it would be good to bear in mind that in the rest of the world, the two-thirds (or four-fifths or nine-tenths) society is on the other side.

—NORBERTO BOBBIO
"The Upturned Utopia"
(*Translated by Patrick Camiller*)

(S. E. Upgobkin and A. A. Prelapsarianov are in Heaven, a gloomy, derelict place like a city after an earthquake. They are dressed in high fur hats and greatcoats. Snow falls on them. They are seated on wooden crates. Between them is another crate they are using as a table. They are playing cards.

A samovar stands on a fourth crate, brewing tea.)

SERGE ESMERELDOVICH UPGOBKIN
I spent my many years on earth loud in proclaiming the faith that there is no God.

ALEKSII ANTEDILLUVIANOVICH PRELAPSAPIANOV
Now you have been dead almost ten years. What do you think now?

SERGE ESMERELDOVICH UPGOBKIN
I am bewildered. I expected more from the Afterlife, in the way of conclusive proof, in some form or another . . .

ALEKSII ANTEDILLUVIANOVICH PRELAPSAPIANOV
But the Ancient of Days remains evasive, ineffable, in Heaven as on earth.

Heaven, I had been led to believe in my childhood, was not such a dark and gloomy place, which forces upon me the suspicion that my mother *lied* to me each night as I

knelt by my bed, praying; a suspicion I cannot entertain.
Your deal.

SERGE ESMERELDOVICH UPGOBKIN
And I must admit I am tired of playing cards with you,
Aleksii Antedilluvianovich.

ALEKSII ANTEDILLUVIANOVICH PRELAPSAPIANOV
I believe I have improved my card game considerably,
Serge Esmereldovich.

SERGE ESMERELDOVICH UPGOBKIN
After ten years of playing, Aleksii, it would actually be
more interesting to me if your game had *not* improved.
Can we think of nothing else to do?

ALEKSII ANTEDILLUVIANOVICH PRELAPSAPIANOV
We could look down on the earth, see how things are going
for Russia.

(Little pause.)

SERGE ESMERELDOVICH UPGOBKIN
Let's not.

ALEKSII ANTEDILLUVIANOVICH PRELAPSAPIANOV
Your deal.

SERGE ESMERELDOVICH UPGOBKIN
Tea?

(Aleksii nods "yes"; Serge gets the tea.)

ALEKSII ANTEDILLUVIANOVICH PRELAPSAPIANOV

We could look down on the earth and see how things are going elsewhere. Cuba. Rwanda. Bosnia. Pakistan. (*Beat*) Afghanistan?

SERGE ESMERELDOVICH UPGOBKIN

God forbid.

ALEKSII ANTEDILLUVIANOVICH PRELAPSAPIANOV

Yes, perhaps not. It is *depressing*.

SERGE ESMERELDOVICH UPGOBKIN

It is *very* depressing.

ALEKSII ANTEDILLUVIANOVICH PRELAPSAPIANOV

It is.

SERGE ESMERELDOVICH UPGOBKIN

(*Getting very frustrated*) I had at least expected to see, if not the face of God or the face of Absolute Nothingness, then the Future, at least the Future: But ahead there is only a great cloud of turbulent midnight, and not even the dead can see what is to come.

(*Vodya Domik enters.*)

ALEKSII ANTEDILLUVIANOVICH PRELAPSAPIANOV

(*Moved, sad, wondering*) Look, Serge, a child has come.

SERGE ESMERELDOVICH UPGOBKIN

Hello little girl.

VODYA DOMIK

Hello.

ALEKSII ANTEDILLUVIANOVICH PRELAPSAPIANOV

How sad to see a little one wandering Night's Plutonian
Shore.

VODYA DOMIK

Plutonium? Is there plutonium even here?

ALEKSII ANTEDILLUVIANOVICH PRELAPSAPIANOV

No, no, *Plutonian-n-n-n*, not plutonium-m-m-m. I was
quoting the great American poet, Edgar Allan Poe.

SERGE ESMERELDOVICH UPGOBKIN

I prefer Emerson. So dialectical! But moral and spiritual
too, like Dostoevsky. If Dostoevsky had lived in America,
and had had a sunnier disposition, he might have been
Emerson. They were contemporaries. The world is fantas-
tical! I miss it so.

ALEKSII ANTEDILLUVIANOVICH PRELAPSAPIANOV

(To Vodya) Welcome to Nevermore.

SERGE ESMERELDOVICH UPGOBKIN

How did you die, child?

VODYA DOMIK

Cancer, a wild profusion of cells; dark flowerings in my
lungs, my brain, my blood, my bones; dandelion and
morning glory vine seized and overwhelmed the field; life
in my body ran riot. And here I am.

ALEKSII ANTEDILLUVIANOVICH PRELAPSAPIANOV
I died from speaking too much.

SERGE ESMERELDOVICH UPGOBKIN
I died from leaping.

ALEKSII ANTEDILLUVIANOVICH PRELAPSAPIANOV
He leapt, he died, and still he cannot see the New.

SERGE ESMERELDOVICH UPGOBKIN
It is bitter.

VODYA DOMIK
The socialist experiment in the Soviet Union has failed, grandfathers.

ALEKSII ANTEDILLUVIANOVICH PRELAPSAPIANOV
It has.

VODYA DOMIK
And what sense are we to make of the wreckage?
Perhaps the principles were always wrong. Perhaps it is true that social justice, economic justice, equality, community, an end to master and slave, the withering away of the state: These are desirable but not realizable on the earth. (*Little pause.*)
Perhaps the failure of socialism in the East speaks only of the inadequacy and criminal folly of any attempt to organize more equitably and rationally the production and distribution of the wealth of nations. And chaos, market fluctuations, rich and poor, colonialism and war are all that we shall ever see.

(Little pause.)

Perhaps, even, the wreckage that became the Union of Soviet Socialist Republics is so dreadful to contemplate that the histories and legends of Red October, indeed of hundreds of years of communitarian, millenarian and socialist struggle, will come to seem mere prelude to Stalin, the gulags, the death of free thought, dignity and human decency; and "socialist" become a foul epithet; and to the ravages of Capital there will be no conceivable alternative.

ALEKSII ANTEDILLUVIANOVICH PRELAPSAPIANOV
It is bitter.

SERGE ESMERELDOVICH UPGOBKIN
It is very bitter.

VODYA DOMIK
I am inexpressibly sad, grandfathers. Tell me a story.

(Little pause.)

SERGE ESMERELDOVICH UPGOBKIN
I have this one story, a Russian story . . .

ALEKSII ANTEDILLUVIANOVICH PRELAPSAPIANOV
Whatever they do, whatever the glory or ignominy, as we move through history, Russians make great stories.

SERGE ESMERELDOVICH UPGOBKIN
I have this one story, but I can say only that it happened, and not what it means:
(Vodya climbs up on his lap.)

SERGE ESMERELDOVICH UPGOBKIN

Vladimir Ilyich Ulyanov was very sad. He was seventeen years old, and the secret police had just hanged his brother Sasha, for having plotted to kill the Czar. All this was long ago. Because he already missed his brother very much, Vladimir, who was to become Great Lenin, decided to read his brother's favorite book: a novel, by Chernyshevsky, the title and contents of which asked the immortal question; which Lenin asked and in asking stood the world on its head; the question which challenges us to both contemplation and, if we love the world, to action; the question which implies: Something is terribly wrong with the world, and avers: Human beings can change it; the question asked by the living and, apparently, by the fretful dead as well:

What is to be done?

(Little pause.)

VODYA DOMIK

What *is* to be done?

ALEKSII ANTEDILLUVIANOVICH PRELAPSAPIANOV

Yes. What is to be done?

END

TWO POEMS
▼

AN EPITHALAMION

For Steven and
Susan Gochenour-Rosen

En su llama mortal la luz te envuelve.
(The light wraps you in its mortal flame.)

—PABLO NERUDA
"En Su Llama Mortal"
(Translated by W. S. Merwin)

I. Design

Here then is the Design, an imposition which,
like any imposition, must rankle, has to be
resisted
even if, as we do now,
it calls on us to celebrate—
for what is life without Design?

Mere anarchy, that state of black
geographilessness,
a house too big to rattle in
without a fear of loss
or getting lost . . .

We need a System,
of roads, of compass points, of up and down,
and now and then,
a Highway Sign, arc-lit emerald-bright
against the dark of sky at night:

Which sign reads: We
are here, and probably,
down this path there lies a point
towards which we want, but not too soon,
to go.

Celebrate Design then, let's!
The intricate arabesques, the curved, flowering branches of
an improbable symmetrical tree,

word and ritual and public vow,
timely impositions on
the ineffable anarchic love

that blossoms madly in these hearts.

II. HOUSES

1.
We'll build a little Dutch House,
somber geometry of liberality and justice,
warmth, comfort and the common good,
planes of dark, polished wood
and thick cool walls,
generous surfaces to catch
the everywhere-falling white
plaster and amber light.

2.
our house will be
as a Japanese house

tangible, in a world
of fearsome drifting illusion

but not too tangible

translucent screens
of paper and wood

the cold is welcome,
    it does not frighten us

and low lacquered tables to mirror back
the scattered and the ghostly light.

3.
In our French house we dance
minuets,
       ma minette,
          aerial duets
in candelabra light,
the heaviest thoughts are infused, made
buoyant, float like stones to the ceiling,
ALOFT, borne up by our elegant helium joy.
The soft light of tapers illumines us there.

4.
Or we'll inhabit a tent in the desert.
Muezzins hosanna to Allah at sunset,
their long cries the shifting design of the dunes,
the dying sun-side burnished, hot peach;
lead-cold mauve in the obverse, shadows of spoon.
Cloth-house for nomads,
for portage by camel and starlight at night,

oh what a practical turtle-affair,
this nomad domesticity, traveling light.

The sand floor patterned in waves by the wind,
the faint smell of water where
no water is . . .

5.
. . . in our little German Haus
We dwell as Jews do, uneasily, but
Mad for the art und the music that's there . . .

6.
In our Spanish house,

the rustle of the olive groves,
the light as it moves through the leaves,
which silver it.

The oranges:
little sprays of scented mist cloud out
where our greedy fingers tear the skins . . .

Waves lap and crash against the bedroom door.
We wait and listen and dream of seafood.

And exchange tearing, torn, Moorish
Mediterranean looks:

     In the lemonlit bedroom, my own Spanish lover,
     Eruptions reflect.
     Perched above the sea.
     In your kiss I taste sea-salt,
     Rainbow-shot, citrus, not
          unlike the savor of somebody's tears.

     Not mine, I hope!

7.
Our rock and roughcast Finnish hut stands
In woods of Arctic Pine.
Giant, raggedy black trees,
shagged by the coldest winds, outside.

The black pines sway:
The breathing of winter that travels leagues,
Across barren wastes from Russia-way.

We are warm inside, in bed, in sweaters,
Finnish sweaters: Knobby Wool
Of some tough sheep.

Thump! Thump!
Outside elk and reindeer bump their noses
against the stones of the bedroom wall.
Envious Elk! You know but cannot feel
the warmth within, and so you bump your snouts,
you fearful, dull-horned ruminants!

Dazzled by the midnight cascading auroras
all around your antlered heads;
underneath your delicate hooves,
the ice aflame with Northern Lights.

8.
Our house is the scandal of the neighborhood,
the work of a well-traveled lunatic architect.

(He) (I) love(s) You! Come plump up the nest!
Our parabled parabola of twigs, grasses, mud,
of newspaper shreddings, the stories of our lives,

and of our life together

and neon-blue feathers to shine in the light!

III. ADVICE FROM A FRIEND

1.
Trust each other, completely, entirely, trust like an animal, trust even more than that, raze every barricade, every obstacle to trust. Be relentless, leave no stone unturned, trust each other. Know with absolute deathless certainty that your lover wishes nothing but that all is well with you. Do you know that? Do you know that your lover is more trustworthy than even you yourself are? If not, work harder, know it, this is important, not even your mother can be trusted half as much. That's one thing.

2.
Be understanding. Be more than that. Merge entirely your being with your lover's life. Have the same dreams at night. And yet, keep a healthy distance always; no one likes feeling crowded.

3.
Your lover complains, or is sad. Listen attentively to each ululation, to each keening note of your lover's lament. What matter if you've heard it all before, only last week, only last night even, and you're bored? Listen as though your lover had sat down and delivered a spontaneous exegesis on Grief worthy of Montaigne or Browne or Emerson. Find different kinds of listening expressions, too, be inventive,

and be careful that the look you imagine expressive of rapt attentiveness isn't becoming a glazed fixed stare.

4.

Listen, trust, accommodate, placate, soothe. Be available, enthusiastic, supportive, generous, surprising, sexy, mysterious, challenging. Be a teacher, a pupil, a nurse, a good patient. A child a parent analysand and analyst both, be a true mirror and a flattering portrait both, be an adorable house pet, household god, father-confessor, mother-intercessor, your lover's favorite relative, favorite movie star, favorite food, share everything, hide nothing, (but remember mysterious and sexy, see ABOVE), see everything, overlook faults, speak frankly but encouragingly always and, if this proves difficult or

5.

impossible

6.

throw plates, smash furniture, shout abuse. Disturb the neighbors, poison the fishbowls, drown the plants, destroy each other's diaries after reading them and scissor each other's socks, celebrate with barbaric obstreperousness, with bonfires and war cries and cannibal stares the indestructible cast iron certainty of what we fuse in the name of that wild endeavor, that ecstatic bellicose enterprise, love.

IV. A WEDDING CELEBRATION TWENTY-EIGHT MILES FROM BOSTON ON A HOT JULY EVENING, WITH FIREWORKS AND A BAND

In white wood gazebos the gamps and the yahoos drink
lemonade punch laced with something illegal.

The evening goes forth in a chemical hue of a scarcely
    conceivable
harloty-purple. It's an evening in July twenty-eight miles
    from Boston
and the band in the forest is warming up the weather.

Fireflies phosphoresce their greenystreaks of light
while zillions of bugs thrum mechanically under. The sky is

stars.

Gazebos adjust to the strain of the guests:
Beef-fed Americans! And all the protein in the world's
Inside them! They CELEBRATE! MARRIAGE!
A Wedding of Friends!

The band is a bastion; certified Yankee,
Uncounterfeitable Pilgrim and Puritan
Company Stock:
The brass glitters brass in the star-glittery night,
the conductress hoists her white-wood baton:

Playing loud for America, loud for America, for spacious
    magenta
and star-clotted skies, a wild Whitmaniac oratoriomusic,

Tony Kushner

orobund/orobusto/operatic/and vatic,
gallumphs the exuberant windorchestra, yes!
while contra-pa-luntally minor, the dark
easterly wind of the keen clarinetto
cuts melanchollosally into the Sousa;

the tart cuts the sugar like lemonade punch!

The guests dance, the music drives them,
the guests dance athletically; the green lawn is flattened.

The stars give way to the moon.
A silver dollar minted of mother-of-pearl would look as
    this moon does:
through the rest of the night it will rise and then drop.

It wanders the treetops, searching out
the breathing spaces between leaf, leaf and branch,
a nest for itself in the darkling woods.

When suddenly,
                A Fireworks Display!

spatters the sky with combustion, with
dragon emission.
The fireflies burn green with jealousy and expire at the sight.
The thrumming insect engine retires for the night.

The guests retire to the nearby inn,
their feet sore from dancing,
their bellies contented,
their heads overslopping with laced lemonade.

And dream:
High over Boston a dragon's whirling, chasing his tail,
spinning fire like a welder,

a gold ring of fire in the New England sky.

While elsewhere two hearts beat
a tender triumphal, in
unison, bed in a shadowy place.

Smoke trails linger
sulphur and silver
perfume the dawn
a faint sweet residue . . .

V. Vows

1.
Conjunction, assemblage, congress, union:
Life isn't meant to be lived alone.
A life apart is a desperate fiction.
Life is an intermediate business:
a field of light bordered by love,
a sea of desire stretched between shores.

Marriage is the strength of union.
Marriage is the harmonic blend.
Marriage is the elegant dialectic of counterpoint.
Marriage is the faultless, fragile logic of ecology:
  A reasonable process of give and take
   unfolding through cyclical and linear time.

A wedding is the conjoining of systems in which
neither loses its single splendor and both are completely
transformed. As, for example,

> The dawn is the wedding of the Night and the Day,
> and is neither, and both,
> and is, in itself, the most beautiful time,
> abundant artless beauty,
> free and careless magnificence.

2.

Encircled by this breathing world
within this close sphere of warm summer night
ringed by this congress of friends here assembled
we make declaration of our love and our union
in public declaring what's privately ours.
From this crowd of hearts, shared heat and blood.

3.

I am yours, who I love, not a dream but life, not fantasy,
immortality, eternity, but the present moment and all-too-
mortal flesh; to what is hardest; love is hardest; hard and
simple and what is best in life.

Love care honor growth—fine simple things and I make a
vow of them to you.

I too vow these to you who I also love and also to the
careful protecting and preserving of dreams. Circle within
circle, concentrically guarded, in the pliable element of
the innermost heart, a garden blossoms in a golden ring;
the dream of dawn in paradise shines there. Love is
imagination's spur and food.

I promise you a future, impossible things, Justice and freedom and life without loss,

a practical pillow, a home, in fact, a sheltering and with-
standing spirit and always a room for your dreaming.

4.
Light is the Wedding of Matter and Spirit,
wave and particle, it is neither and both,
and is in itself the blood of creation.
It floods across galaxies and has no end,
it describes and transforms with a single motion.

May our love be as light.

VI. AND THEN . . .

Together, old and content,
the day is warm and nearly over, the first breeze of
    evening
plays in your hair. The sun sinks behind us,
silhouetting the city.
An old hand is ringing down the curtain.
We cross the bridge that goes east
into night.

THE SECOND MONTH
OF MOURNING

1.
I had to, I felt it
necessary to, meaning no
disrespect out of love only
out of love
only I felt it needed
to be done that I had to
necessary this remove this
stone, this barring rock.

Boulder heavy dispatching the duty of
obstructing I had to
for the free flow

for the free flow again
of the air.

Naught else, otherwise.

2.
You, or
the loss of you.

You, or
the loss of you.

Now what

Now what kind of a choice
you
or the loss of you
is
that?

Now you, or
rather, the loss of you
is all the you there is,
and so,
now,
you *are* the loss of you.

Or, rather . . .

No way to say this I can't
no way to say
no way.

3.
Human beings are
human beings are funny animals when

confronted with the loss of
with loss, they
make sounds of distress
they make sounds of distress comical
when viewed
objectively.
Catalogue:

4.
Transparent liquid seepage
from mucous membrane,
duct, gland.
General leaking from facial holes.
Dissolved saline, salt water,
a bathing of the epidermis with
fever-water warmed in fur-lined caves,
cavities deep within
the cranium tucked
up near the blood-fueled furnace,
the blood-driven engine of grief,
the organ of mourning,
the body part
whose job it is
to order up, to distill
in the visceral alembic the biochemical
perfumes of what it is
to grieve.

To grieve the loss of . . .

5.
And that's why
it's all grey matter upstairs where
the Court of Mourning is held,
its courtiers ashen in mourning-wear grey,
and the lights along the passageways
are dim or all
extinguished.

And every door is carpeted and locked.

And every port and portal, blocked.

And time
is held immobile in the uncirculating air.

It's an airless old archive upstairs where
grey documents are stored important to
an obscure discipline
whose disciples' numbers dwindle:
now less-by-one; by you.

By the subtraction, or
rather by the loss of . . .

6.
. . . The hooting noises and the drowning sounds,
the ferocious sucking in of air against
the inner onrush of some acidic fluid filling up
the passageways water ballooning the lungs
the submarined larynx going
glub

glub
glub
the
strangulated hee-hee-hee bursting into
the mighty BAWL, or
the keen, the trill, the bark,
the wobble, the silly fluting cry,
signaling distress to indifference,
calling loss to absence,
to you or rather
to the loss of you.

Silent, too. How they cry.
Open-mouthed,
contorted,
eyes screwed shut,
hiss of air escaping as whistle
the corkscrewed, shuttered-up throat;
or no hiss at all, no air,
purpura, black spots,
the extravasation of blood,
asphyxiation . . . and their little hands
make little . . . (*gestures*)
in the cold air, little . . . (*gestures*)
their little hands reach up
towards nothing there in the dis-spirited air
and they go . . . (*gestures*)
a little.

It's a gesture
it's a gesture they learned
from the dying.

7.
If the stone
If the rock cannot be moved it can at least
be described.

Soft, grey, spherical, a dead little planet.
Dusty, so it must be
old. It dropped
from the moon.

It should have landed
sploosh into some choppy lead-black icy
deep January sea somewhere far
in the Northern Hemisphere far
from land but instead
the damned thing's dropped
with a placid, almost genial
absolute immobility
an incontrovertible here-ness
right here entirely obstructing
my view of . . .
my view of . . .
Well whatever's on the other side.
I don't
I don't remember what was there.
Who or what
there was to see before
the replacement of that with this
blank, thought-stopping rockface filling
the field of sight.
I don't remember what.

Tony Kushner

Oh yes. Now. You, or
the loss of you. Now,
I remember.

8.
Perhaps patience and time will trace
a transubstantial evolving: a change
of no-hope mineral permanence into
something if not green then at least
vegetable, which withers, or perhaps
animal, which dies:
rock acquiring a kind of lumbering organicity,
bursitic, deliberate,
elephantine, ox-ponderous,
an obedient beast
of a nearly insupportable
burden,
some kind of gentle, domesticated animal that,
when prodded, lopes, and
moos

and waves its head like a conductor's hand
in slow graceful arcs,
down beat, from side to side
metronome mapping of a largo-land,
a broad terrain where activity
tends towards halting, rocks
towards cessation
between breath and breath.

9.

In August
I saw the deathroom angels at their work,
intent over your body, dismantling.
With their tin pails and brushes,
rusty tools,
with creaking joists and pulleys,
with thick braided rope, in the silent hum
of their serious industry,
bathed in the shadowless chemical light of extraction
the deathroom angels plied their trade,
standing like tombstones, in pools of tears.

And for this once they were efficient,
and though hardly merciful they were
mercifully brief.

Watching them
in the industrial cold
of the deathbed room:
their grey intelligent faces,
their nimble, practiced fingers,
their terrible strong hands,
the stained canvas of their stiff grey gowns,
bowed under in the vascular pulse of the fluorescent
    lamps,
their song . . .
gleaned from the hum of their serious industry:
Intent over you . . .

Oh but stay.
Oh but stay.
Oh but stay . . . away from that.
Oh but stay away from
that.
Draw down the heavy shade
to shield that scene.

10.
A scaly talon sinks its
sixteenpenny galvanized iron
nails into the soft and bloody
tissue of my all-but-unresisting heart.
Pain feels like a blow
at first—Whose fist is it—
till nerves vivify and start to scream to
Life.
Eventually,
an accommodation of sorts.
Not
now.

11.
A rose for the rose quarter.
You were desperate
to say something or write
something and you went . . . *(gestures)*
but when finally with pen in hand you
or the pain or the fear or the medication wrote
only poetry:

To find some way to say . . .

As the deathroom angels sang all about you,
plying their trade, those grim professionals:

You wrote:
A rose for the rose quarter
and said:
It would be nice
to be able to say
enough.

And anyone watching would have to agree.

And on the sleepless night
after the service
when a semitropical cloudburst broke
drowning the impossible day,

I saw you
atop that bare little hill,
hospital gown for a winding sheet,
knees drawn up,
arms on knees, head
in hands and the rain
beat down and you,
confused,
asked this question:
"What is this?
What's this?"
and I still have no way
no way to answer you, or

rather, to answer
the loss of you.

12.
Enough.

No way to end this,
no way to make an end.

You, or
the loss of you.

Now what kind of a choice
is that?

You, or
the loss of you.

And what if the rock can't be budged?
And what if never again the free flow of the air?

And now you are the loss of you.

In a cold dead August down in the infernal South,
we blinked dry bloody eyes against the cinder-wind,
watching
while fire ants threaded tunnels,
red veins through the earth of your grave.

A PRAYER

▼

*This prayer for the Episcopalian
National Day of Prayer for AIDS was
delivered at the Cathedral Church
of St. John the Divine
in New York City on
October 9, 1994.*

Dearly Beloved: Today is a National Day of Prayer for AIDS. Let us pray.

God:

A cure would be nice. Rid those infected by this insatiable unappeasable murderer of its lethal presence. Reconstitute the shattered, restore to health all those whose bodies, beleaguered, have betrayed them, whose defenses have permitted entrance to illnesses formerly at home only in cattle, in swine and in birds. Return to the cattle, the swine and the birds the intestinal parasite, the invader of lungs, the eye-blinder, the brain-devourer, the detacher of retinas. Rid even the cattle and birds of these terrors; heal the whole world. Now. Now. Now. Now.

Grant us an end that is not fatal. Protect: the injection-drug user, the baby with AIDS, the sex worker, the woman whose lover was infected, the gay man whose lover was infected; protect the infected lover, protect the casual contact, the one-night stand, the pickup, the put-down, protect the fools who don't protect themselves, who don't protect others: YOU protect them. The misguided, too and the misinformed, the ambivalent about living, show them life, not death; the kid who thinks that immortality is part of the numinous glory of sex. Who didn't believe this, once,

discovering sex? Everyone did. Protect this kid, let this kid
learn otherwise, and live past the learning; protect all kids,
make them wiser but, until wise, make them immortal.

Enlighten the unenlightened: The Pope, the cardinals,
archbishops and priests, even John O'Connor, teach him
how Christ's kindness worked: Remind him, he's forgotten, make them all remember, replace the ice water in
their veins with the blood of Christ, let it pound in their
temples: The insurance executive as well as the priest,
the congressional representative, the Justice and the judge,
the pharmaceutical profiteer, the doctor, the cop, the
anchorwoman and the televangelist, make their heads throb
with memory, make them see with new eyes Christ's
wounds as K.S. lesions, Christ's thin body AIDS-thin, his
shrunken chest pneumonia-deflated, his broken limbs,
his pierced hands: stigmata of this unholy plague. Let the
spilled blood which angels gathered, Christ's blood be
understood: It is shared and infected blood.

Even John O'Connor, even Bob Dole, Giuliani and Gingrich,
Jesse Helms and Pat Robertson—tear open their hearts,
let them burn with compassion, stun them with understanding, ravish their violent, politick, cynical souls, make
them wiser, better, braver people. You can. You, after all,
are God. This is not too much to ask.

Grant us an end to this pandemic: Why, after all, a pandemic? Why now? Give aid to the needy, not AIDS, give
assistance to those seeking justice, not further impediment.
Find some other way to teach us your lessons; we're eager
to learn, we are only reluctant to die.

Bring back our dead, all our dead, give us certain knowledge of the future recovery of all those we've lost, restitution of all those we've lost, in Paradise if not on earth, but guarantee it. Don't ask faith of people who have lost so much. Don't *dare*.

Manifest yourself now. With a cure, now. With a treatment, now. With a treatment that isn't more snakebite venom, more spiderbite poison, which is all that fourteen years of prayers and waiting and searching have given us. Reveal yourself with an imminent medical miracle. Announce it on the evening news: something, finally, that doesn't fail to live up to its promise by morning of the following day. Reagan is gone, more or less, and Bush is gone, and Nixon and the Cold War are finally gone, and apartheid is gone, but AIDS is still here. And we are waiting. For the end of it.

Hear our prayer.

Must grace fall so unevenly on the earth? Must goodness precipitate so lightly, so infrequently from sky to parched ground? We are your crop, your sprouted seed, the harvest perishes in its faith for you for lack of lively rain.

Your silence, I must tell you, so steadfastly maintained, even in the face of our appalling need, is outrageous.

I speak now not for those assembled here but for myself, from the considerable rage that vexes my heart. So many have died this year alone: In case you were absent, God, or absent-minded, may I mention a few of them, commend their ends to your accounting?

A Prayer

Randy Shilts, Jeff Schmalz, Paul Walker, Mary Darling, Harry Kondoleon, Bill Anderson, Ron Vawter, Tim Melester, Paul Monette.

Let each name stand for ten thousand more, and a hundred thousand others will remain unnoted. And many more are sick and have worsened; they take flight in number, I've noticed, they travel multiply, in flocks, like birds, these critically ill: Having heard the call of a general departing, they test their wings, the thermal currents, fighting for updrafts to carry them to, or carry them from, life. Here is courage and will and imagination and tenacity. Where, God, are you?

Your silence, again, is outrageous to me, it places you impossibly among the ranks of the monstrously indifferent, no better than a Washington politician, no better than an Albany Republican, Alfonse D'Amato, something that meager, that immured against Justice.

Where you must not be placed. Must grace fall so unevenly on the earth? Must goodness precipitate from sky to ground so infrequently? We are parched for goodness, we perish for lack of lively rain; there's a drought for want of grace, everywhere. Surely this has not escaped your notice? All life hesitates now, wondering: in the night which has descended, in the dry endless night that's fallen instead of the expected rain: Where are you?

One of the Hasidim, Menachem Mendl of Kotsk, sealed himself up in a hermitage, and for an entire year refused to answer the pleas of his disciples; would not respond when they knocked at his door, would not answer no matter how hard they knocked; their repeated inquiries after his health did not elicit a single response, their concern produced only silence, their bewilderment, their grief, their fears that he had died behind the door of his cell—for a year they heard nothing from Menachem Mendl of Kotsk.

And then one day he emerged from his cell. His door stood open, and there he was. His disciples demanded an explanation. He told them: "Now perhaps you understand my relationship with the Almighty, who will not reveal Himself no matter how hard I beg, who hides His face from me."

Except one must mention: They had only a year to wait, those tormented, aggrieved disciples, and then they had answers, and explanations. The analogy fails. We've waited a decade and a half for your help. We have ashes, and graves, and grief so overtopping it can no longer be recognized as grief, but has become a kind of dark amazement that so much can be endured; you hide your face from us.

I've been to the Wailing Wall, and I watched men and women daven, as they'd been davening for centuries, Jews before the impassive wall of history, believing their rocking could melt or move those great stones, believing that the messages they stick in the cracks could travel somehow to the other side. The anchorites, too, in the Syrian Desert, would weep over rocks, committed to dissolving the stones with their tears. Is prayer mere attrition, a kind of endurance?

A Prayer

If prayer is a beseeching, a seeking after the hidden heart and face of God, then this peremptory, querulous, insistent demanding, this pounding at your door cannot be called a prayer, this importunate sleeve-tugging while you are distracted—concerned, perhaps with something more important, holding the earth to its orbit, perhaps, keeping it from careening into the sun; or perhaps you tend another world other than ours, and do a better job with that one, where there is nothing like AIDS, and your tutelage is gentler, and the lessons are easier to learn.

Four years ago a thirty-one-year-old woman named Milagros Martinez drowned herself off the shore of upper Manhattan Island. Infected with the virus, she went to the river and threw her body, which had become a fearful thing to her, her enemy now, she threw her body and the soul it housed into the Hudson, ending her life. Before she drowned, from the edge of drowning, she called to her son, seven years old: She'd left him standing on the riverbank. According to police, and the sixty-seven-word newspaper article that is, as far as I know, her only memorial, Milagros Martinez begged her son to join her in the water, but the child refused, watching instead as his mother was taken, by tributary currents, to some dark, unknowable bed.

What's become of the child of Milagros Martinez? Where is he now? What dreams does he have, what river courses through his dreams at night? What bodies does it bear? From what raging sea is that river flowing, and toward what conceivable future?

I am in the habit of hoping. But it's become wrong to draw hope from this conflagration. If holocaust alone is the only lesson we attend to, then what bat-winged butcher angel is our teacher, and towards what conceivable future, along the banks of what river of the dead, do we make our way?

I am in the habit of asking small things of you: one of the guilty who hasn't done enough, one of the lucky, the survivors by accident. When I was ten an uncle told me you didn't exist: "We descend from apes," he said, "the universe will end, and there is no God." I believed the ape part—my uncle had thick black hair on his arms and knuckles, so apes was easy—and the universe become a nulliverse, that too was scary fun. And since his well-meaning instruction I have not *known* your existence, as some friends of mine do; but you have left bread-crumb traces inside of me. Rapacious birds swoop down and the traces are obscured, but the path is recoverable. It can be discovered again.

So a cure for AIDS. For racism too. For homophobia and sexism, and an end to war, to nationalism and capitalism, to work as such and to hatred of the flesh. Restore the despoiled world, end the pandemic of breast cancer too, bring back Danitra Vance, and Audre Lorde, and Sigrid Wurschmidt, dead at thirty-six, and my mother, dead at sixty-five. Or at least guarantee that loss is not irrecoverable, so that life can be endured. But above all, since this is my job today, a cure.

If you cannot do these things for us, we will do them for ourselves, but slowly, because we can't see far ahead. At least give us the time to accomplish the future. We had a pact; you engendered us. Don't expect that we will forgive you if you allow us to be endangered. Forgiveness, too, is a lesson loss doesn't teach.

I almost know you are there. I think you are our home. At present we are homeless, or imagine ourselves to be. Bleeding life in the universe of wounds. Be thou more sheltering, God. Pay more attention.

About the Author

Tony Kushner's plays include *A Bright Room Called Day; The Illusion,* freely adapted from Corneille; *Angels in America, A Gay Fantasia on National Themes, Part One: Millennium Approaches* and *Part Two: Perestroika;* and adaptations of Goethe's *Stella,* Brecht's *The Good Person of Setzuan* and Ansky's *The Dybbuk.* His work has been produced by theatres throughout the United States and *Angels in America* has been produced in over thirty countries. Mr. Kushner is the recipient of numerous awards, including the 1993 Pulitzer Prize for Drama. He was born in Manhattan and grew up in Lake Charles, Louisiana.